JUMP START PHP

BY CALLUM HOPKINS

Jump Start PHP

by Callum Hopkins

Copyright © 2013 SitePoint Pty. Ltd.

Product Manager: Simon Mackie   **English Editor:** Paul Fitzpatrick
Technical Editor: Timothy Boronczyk   **Cover Designer:** Alex Walker

sitepoint

Published by SitePoint Pty. Ltd.

48 Cambridge Street Collingwood
VIC Australia 3066
Web: www.sitepoint.com
Email: business@sitepoint.com

ISBN 978-0-9874674-0-9 (print)

ISBN 978-0-9874674-1-6 (ebook)
Printed and bound in the United States of America

About Callum Hopkins

Callum is a web developer by trade and a designer by passion. Armed with knowledge in both design and development processes, he is able to influence both sides of the web building process. His passion for complex coding functions and beautiful design and functionality drives him to seek out new ways to build, design and optimize web based solutions for clients around the world.

About SitePoint

SitePoint specializes in publishing fun, practical, and easy-to-understand content for web professionals. Visit http://www.sitepoint.com/ to access our blogs, books, newsletters, articles, and community forums. You'll find a stack of information on JavaScript, PHP, Ruby, mobile development, design, and more.

About Jump Start

Jump Start books provide you with a rapid and practical introduction to web development languages and technologies. Typically around 150 pages in length, they can be read in a weekend, giving you a solid grounding in the topic and the confidence to experiment on your own.

*To all my family and friends,
thank you for your continued
support, and I love you all.*

Table of Contents

Preface..xi

Who Should Read This Book...................................xi

Conventions Used..xi

    Code Samples..xi

    Tips, Notes, and Warnings.............................xiii

Supplementary Materials...................................xiii

Do You Want to Keep Learning?...........................xiv

Chapter 1   Server Kick-Start....................49

What is PHP?...1

Setting Up...2

Getting Started...3

    Windows...3

    Mac OS X..6

    Linux...9

PHP Configuration...11

Hello PHP World...13

PHP Variables...16

Arrays...19

Comments..20

Preparing Our Project...21

Summary..22

Chapter 2   PHP & Data............................23

Operators...23

Conditional Statements.......................................25

if Statement 25

else Statement 25

elseif Statement 26

switch Statement 26

Loops 28

for Loop 28

while Loop 29

foreach 29

Databases, MySQL, and PHP 30

Summary 128

Chapter 3   **Objects and OOP** 41

First Steps in OOP 42

Extending Classes 45

Templates 49

Project Files 52

Summary 58

Chapter 4   **Forms** 61

Form Elements 61

POST and GET 63

Form Action with PHP 69

Superglobals and $_REQUEST 70

Forms and Databases 71

Building on our Platform 74

Summary 128

Chapter 5   **Sessions and Cookies** 89

Cookies: Overview 89

Sessions: Overview 90

Session Vs Cookies 91

    Cookies 91

    Sessions 92

Sessions and Cookies in PHP 93

    Cookies in PHP 93

    Sessions in PHP 95

Project 97

    Summary 128

Chapter 6   **PHP and Security** 121

php.ini and Security 121

    allow_url_include 122

    open_basedir 123

    Error Management 123

    Improving Session Security 124

Validating Submitted Data 126

Summary 128

Conclusion 129

Preface

PHP is considered as one of the most popular web based languages. At its core, PHP was designed to help enhance web pages and make their content dynamic, but over the years PHP has evolved in something much more useful than this. With PHP, developers are easily able to build complex applications, such as forums, picture galleries and a whole lot more.

In this book, *Jump Start PHP*, we will teach you the basics to writing and developing in PHP and will guide from building basic PHP web pages with dynamic content, to building interactive web based applications. We'll address issues such as security, database interaction and setting up developer environments for building your PHP applications.

Throughout *Jump Start PHP*, we will work on an ongoing project, a small but robust blogging application, which will apply the theory discussed in each chapter to a real development scenario. This project will incorporate some useful functionality (a front-end to display posts, comments, and administrative tools) and will hopefully help to demonstrate the concepts we discuss throughout the book

Who Should Read This Book

Developers seeking a rapid introduction to PHP. You'll need to know HTML and CSS, and experience with other programming languages would be useful.

Conventions Used

You'll notice that we've used certain typographic and layout styles throughout this book to signify different types of information. Look out for the following items.

Code Samples

Code in this book will be displayed using a fixed-width font, like so:

```
<h1>A Perfect Summer's Day</h1>
<p>It was a lovely day for a walk in the park. The birds
were singing and the kids were all back at school.</p>
```

If the code is to be found in the book's code archive, the name of the file will appear at the top of the program listing, like this:

```
                                                                    example.css
.footer {
  background-color: #CCC;
  border-top: 1px solid #333;
}
```

If only part of the file is displayed, this is indicated by the word *excerpt*:

```
                                                            example.css (excerpt)
  border-top: 1px solid #333;
```

If additional code is to be inserted into an existing example, the new code will be displayed in bold:

```
function animate() {
  new_variable = "Hello";
}
```

Also, where existing code is required for context, rather than repeat all the code, a ⋮ will be displayed:

```
function animate() {
  ⋮
  return new_variable;
}
```

Some lines of code are intended to be entered on one line, but we've had to wrap them because of page constraints. A ➥ indicates a line break that exists for formatting purposes only, and should be ignored.

```
URL.open("http://www.sitepoint.com/responsive-web-design-real-user-
➥testing/?responsive1");
```

Tips, Notes, and Warnings

Hey, You!

Tips will give you helpful little pointers.

Ahem, Excuse Me ...

Notes are useful asides that are related—but not critical—to the topic at hand. Think of them as extra tidbits of information.

Make Sure You Always ...

... pay attention to these important points.

Watch Out!

Warnings will highlight any gotchas that are likely to trip you up along the way.

Supplementary Materials

http://www.sitepoint.com/books/jsphp11/
The book's website, containing links, updates, resources, and more.

https://github.com/spbooks/JSPHP1
The downloadable code archive for this book.

http://www.sitepoint.com/forums/forumdisplay.php?34-PHP
SitePoint's forums, for help on any tricky web problems.

books@sitepoint.com
Our email address, should you need to contact us for support, to report a problem, or for any other reason.

Do You Want to Keep Learning?

You can now get unlimited access to courses and ALL SitePoint books at Learnable for one low price. Enroll now and start learning today! Join Learnable and you'll stay ahead of the newest technology trends: http://www.learnable.com.

Server Kick-Start

What is PHP?

PHP is the most popular sever-side scripting language in web development, powering an estimated 78.9% of all websites.

It was created by Rasmus Lerdorf in 1995, and the name was originally an acronym of "Personal Home Page (Tools)", although now it's better known for the recursive acronym "PHP: Hypertext Preprocessor". The language is managed, monitored, and developed by a group of developers known as The PHP Group, which continues to distribute the scripting language for free through the official PHP website[1].

PHP code is most commonly interpreted, processed, and rendered using a web server with a PHP processor module installed, allowing PHP to be embedded within HTML markup in files with the **.php** extension. In addition, PHP can be deployed on almost every operating system and platform for free, with Linux-based systems being the most popular choice.

---

[1] http://php.net/

Today, PHP development is mainly focused on server-side scripting rather than general-purpose scripting tasks, and it's generally considered to be a competitor to technologies such as Microsoft's ASP.NET, Apache Software Foundation's mod_perl module, and Joyent's Node.js. PHP is primarily used to handle complex data processing that allows dynamic data to appear on web pages, such as math calculations, number crunching, and interacting with a database. It allows developers to take what used to be static HTML content and make it responsive to users' requests, or do the same with permanently-stored data that resides in a database.

PHP has a focus on web development, which makes it an obvious choice for developers when creating web applications or websites. Its gentle learning curve enables developers to quickly start building things in PHP, while the breadth of its features allows developers to expand their projects without resorting to another programming language. Websites such as Digg, Etsy, Yahoo, Facebook, and Wikipedia all use PHP to power sections of their website, including the handling and processing of data related to their visitors.

A simple example of using PHP in a web page is displaying the number of visitors with a counter. A database stores the number of people who have visited the web page, and PHP is used to interact with that database and generate the HTML markup to display the current tally. PHP can also be used to create large, complex, and multi-level navigational websites that have many nested pages, and is commonly used to power ecommerce websites. PHP even allows for the creation of customized experiences for visitors using information gathered about that user.

PHP's popularity has also resulted in a huge community of developers who are willing to offer help to anyone seeking advice and, more often than not, for free, as well as an ever-expanding library of reference material available both online and offline.

Setting Up

PHP is available with almost every shared-server hosting package, and it can also be used alongside Apache HTTP Server software to create a local web server on your home computer. PHP can also be used with your own private web server, which can then be accessed across the Internet.

Local servers on home computers are often set up using the popular LAMP (Linux, Apache, MySQL, and PHP), MAMP (Mac OS X, Apache, MySQL, and PHP), and WAMP (Windows, Apache, MySQL, and PHP) stacks, all of which are available for free download.

These stacks normally comprise of a one-click install program that installs a standard web server setup with default configurations. This allows web developers to set up a local environment that is almost identical to the one provided by their web hosting company. Developers will often start building websites and applications using a local server due to the ease with which they can access working files, and do without the additional time and hassle of uploading files to an online server. In addition, this method means there's no worry that development code will accidentally leak out onto the live site, and developers can also avoid using hosting bandwidth for file transfers.

Getting Started

Getting a local server on your home computer may seem like it could be a complex task, but it's generally fairly simple: a one-click install. There are several options available, depending on which operating system you use:

Windows

With Windows, you have a choice of two popular and powerful installation programs. The first is WAMP[2], a Windows program that installs Apache, PHP, MySQL, and phpMyAdmin on your computer (**phpMyAdmin** is a convenient web-based interface for working with MySQL databases). The other is XAMMP[3] from Apache Friends, a distribution containing Apache, MySQL, PHP, Perl, and phpMyAdmin.

For the purposes of this book, we'll cover setup using WAMP only, but the setup of XAMMP follows a similar process, if you choose to install that package instead.

Your first step is to download WAMP[4]. You'll be given multiple download options, so select the version that corresponds to your computer's processor and operating system version and is "PHP 5.4 2.4".

---

[2] http://www.wampserver.com/en/

[3] http://www.apachefriends.org/en/xampp.html3

[4] http://www.wampserver.com/en/#download-wrapper

Which Processor Do I Have?

To find out which processor you have, look for your "My Computer" icon or alternatively you can head to **Control Panel** and select **System** from the options available. Right-click on it and look for the option **System Type** which should state whether your computer uses a 32 or 64-bit operating system.

 Visual C++

You also need to install Visual C++ 2010 SP1 Re distributable Package x86 or x64 on your computer. The web page will give you links that correspond to your operating system type (32 or 64-bit) and it's highly recommended that you download and install the package on your computer before installing WAMP.

When the download is complete, run the installer program.

Once WAMP has been installed, you should see a new icon in the Windows system tray. The icon for WAMP changes between three different colors that represent the current status of its services:

- Red – Both Apache and MySQL are offline. This could be because they haven't been told to start yet or a fatal configuration issue is preventing them from starting.

- Orange – One of the services failed to start. This usually indicates a minor configuration problem, such as not loading an add-on library correctly or that a default port is in use by another program. It's highly recommended that you seek help from the product's help desk or forums should this happen.

- Green – The services are running and no errors have occurred; all is good.

You can left-click on the WAMP icon and you will be presented with many options for interacting with the services. These options allow you to:

- Manage your Apache and MySQL services

- Switch online/offline

- Install and switch Apache, MySQL, and PHP releases

- Access your log files

- Access your settings files

- Create aliases

Right-clicking on the icon allows you to exit the program, change the program's language, and go to help pages located on WAMP's website. It's recommended that if you are unsure of anything related to the WAMP stack to seek advice from the help files on the WAMP website using the right-click option on the icon.

 Port 80 Problems

The most common issue with WAMP is that port 80 (the port used to connect to the Apache server) may already be in use by another program. If you're running Skype while trying to start up WAMP, for example, you may encounter this error because Skype also uses port 80. To fix it, it's recommended that you close Skype completely and then restart WAMP. There's a solution to this issue on Stack Overflow[5].

To check that the local server is installed and configured correctly, open up your web browser and in its address bar type `localhost` or `127.0.0.1`. You should be greeted with the WAMP home page.

---

[5] http://stackoverflow.com/a/4705033

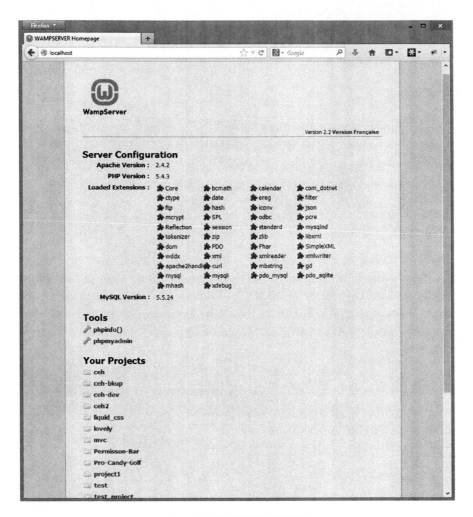

Figure 1.1. The WAMP home page

Mac OS X

For Mac users, there is a simple one-click application for setting up a local server with PHP on your computer called MAMP. As with Windows, you can also use XAMMP, however MAMP is the more popular choice because its development is focused on providing a setup that's perfect for those wishing to develop websites using PHP.

First, you need to download the application from the MAMP website[6] and then, once the file has downloaded, open the **.pkg** file which should initiate the installation process.

MAMP Pro

MAMP may install two folders, one named **MAMP** and the other named **MAMP Pro**. If MAMP Pro is installed on your computer, remove this folder and application. MAMP Pro is a pay-for program, whereas MAMP is a free application.

Once that's done, you can start the MAMP program by clicking on the MAMP icon; you should be welcomed with the splash screen.

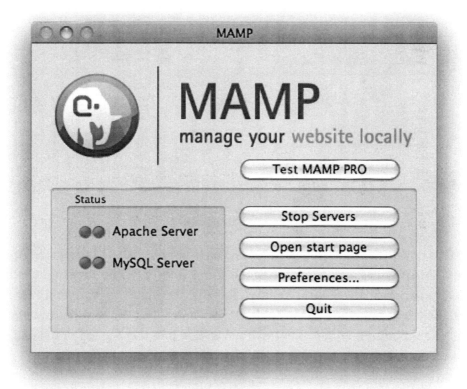

Figure 1.2. The MAMP splash screen

---

[6] http://www.mamp.info/en/index.html

On the splash screen, shown in Figure 1.2, you should see two icons on the left-hand side of the box titled **Apache Server** and **MySQL Server** which should both have red dots next to them. These red dots mean they haven't been started. To fire them up, we need to hit the **Start Servers** button; the dots should switch to green. Shortly after pressing the **Start Servers** button, your default browser should open and load the MAMP start screen.

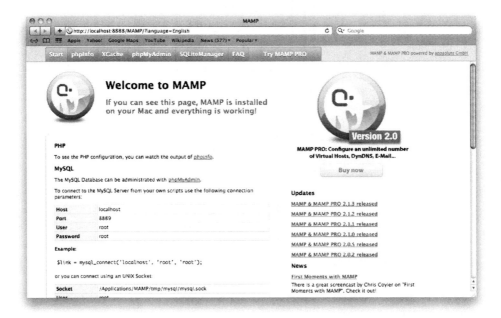

Figure 1.3. MAMP start screen

MAMP is now installed. However, it forces you to use port 8888 to access the Apache server. This is not as nice as accessing the server simply typing `localhost` into the browser's address bar, as WAMP allows. Luckily, there's a very simple fix for this issue. Switch back to the MAMP splash screen and select the **Preferences** button. There should be an option in the small navigation menu at the top of the panel titled **Ports**.

In this window you should see an input box with the label **Apache Port** to the left of it. If you change this option from 8888 to 80 you can now access the MAMP start screen by simply typing `localhost`/`MAMP` into your browser's address bar.

Linux

If you're running a Linux operating system such as Ubuntu or Debian, you can use the terminal to install the LAMP package from the system's repositories. Installing a local server on Linux is slightly different from Windows or Mac OS X. The installation method is a bit more advanced, but it allows a lot more control and freedom when running and managing the server. In fact, the method is almost identical to the one used to manage and run live web servers on Linux. The installation example we'll cover here will specifically show the steps for installing LAMP on Ubuntu.

Your first step is to start the terminal program, which can be done by searching for **Terminal** in Dash Menu, the first icon in the Ubuntu side menu, or by heading to **Applications > Accessories > Terminal** via folder navigation.

Once you have the terminal open, you can start by installing Apache on the computer. You do this by typing the following into the terminal:

```
sudo apt-get install apache2
```

Hit **Enter** and your terminal will start going crazy, but don't panic, this is natural.

Apache should now be installed and the basics of your local server will be set up. To test this, open a web browser and type `localhost` into the address bar. If it has installed successfully, you should be welcomed with the "It works!" splash screen as shown in Figure 1.4.

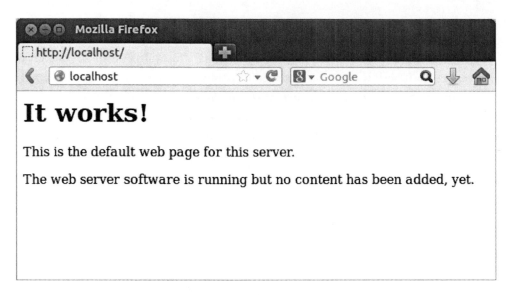

Figure 1.4. Localhost on Linux

Now you'll need to install PHP, so head back to the terminal and type:

```
sudo apt-get install php5 libapache2-mod-php5*
```

PHP 5 will be installed along with the basic libraries it needs to work alongside the Apache server you just installed. Once complete, you have to restart Apache for it to acknowledge PHP was just installed. In the terminal, type the command below:

```
sudo service apache2 restart
```

Your Apache server will now restart, see that you have PHP installed, and will load up all of the libraries needed to run PHP on your local sever.

Now you have your local server up and running and you have PHP installed on it. To install MySQL and phpMyAdmin I recommend following this guide by Mhabub Mamun.[7]

Finally, you have the option to enable the mod_rewrite module for Apache, which allows developers to redirect users to different sections of the website by rewriting the requested URLs. For a full in-depth guide for enabling and settings up the

---

[7] http://www.developmentwall.com/install-apache-php-mysql-phpmyadmin-ubuntu/4

mod_rewrite module, please see the Nettuts+ guide[8], which offers a very detailed step-by-step tutorial.

PHP Configuration

Before we delve into writing some PHP code, let's configure PHP to better suit our project. PHP is configured by the file **php.ini**, which holds all of the core settings relating to how PHP will behave on our server. You can see a quick overview of PHP's current configuration by using the `phpinfo()` function in a PHP script. To do this, create a new file in your server folder named **info.php**, add the following code to the file, and save it:

```php
<?php
        phpinfo();
```

Now, point your browser to the `info.php` file and you should see a page that displays a table full of information about our PHP's current configuration, as shown in Figure 1.5.

---

[8] http://net.tutsplus.com/tutorials/other/a-deeper-look-at-mod_rewrite-for-apache/

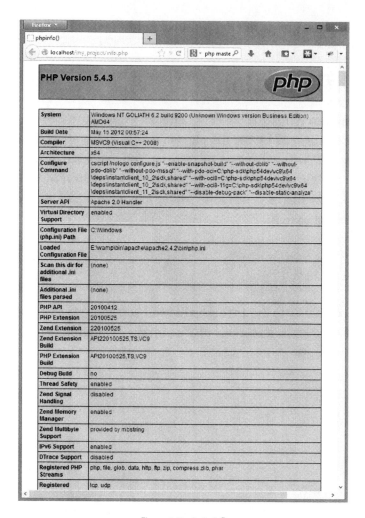

Figure 1.5. phpinfo()

The key thing to find here is the row titled **Configuration File (php.ini) Path** as this will tell you exactly where your **php.ini** file is located. You can see that in Figure 1.5 my **php.ini** file is located at **E\:wamp\bin\apache\apache2.4.2\bin\php.ini**. Your path will very likely be different from this, so use the phpinfo() function to find out what it is.

The **php.ini** file contains a large amount of settings, some of which you may never need to change. However, there are a few which can be changed to help tailor PHP to suit your development style and environment. For a tour of the **php.ini** file, I highly recommend reading the *Tour of php.ini* article I wrote for SitePoint[9].

Hello PHP World

Now that you have your local server installed and running, let's start coding some PHP! We'll start by heading to Apache's web folder, which is located in different places depending on which operating system you are using:

- For Windows users using WAMP, open up Explorer or My Computer and navigate to the directory located at **C:/Program Files/wamp/www/**

- For Mac OS X using MAMP, open Finder and navigate your way to **Applications > MAMP > htdocs** to locate MAMP's web directory.

- The web directory for Linux can be found in /var/www. Many Linux developers like to edit their server's config file to change which directory is used for web files. To do this, please see the solution on Stack Overflow[10].

Once you've found your server's web directory, you need to create a directory to act as your project's "root" directory where all your project files will be located. For now, create a directory named **my_project**. I specifically avoided any spaces or capital letters in the folder's title because it will form part of the URL to access files in this folder.

Now create a new PHP file called **index.php** in the **my_project** folder. Once this file has been created you'll need to open it in a text editor that can edit PHP files.

 ## Choosing a Text Editor

I recommend that you use an editor which supports syntax highlighting for PHP. Choosing an editor is a very personal decision as different editors offer different features; some editors will complement your way of coding and some may conflict with it. In the end, the choice should really depend on which editor makes coding easier and more fun for you. It's also worth trying a few different editors before settling on your final choice.

---

[9] http://www.sitepoint.com/a-tour-of-php-ini/
[10] http://stackoverflow.com/a/5891858

Here's a short list of some of the more popular editors available. It contains a mixture of both free and paid-for editors:

- Adobe Dreamweaver[11] – (Windows and Mac OS X)

  - One of the most well-known editors. It provides a wide range of one-click options and has a built-in FTP client.

- Sublime Text[12] – (Windows, Mac OS X, and Linux)

  - A free-to-try editor which has some powerful shortcuts and macro commands built-in.

- Komodo Edit[13] – (Windows, Mac OS X, and Linux)

  - A powerful free editor with a slick interface and built-in FTP client.

- Coda[14] – (Mac OS X)

  - A very user-friendly editor with a wide range of functionality.

- Notepad++[15] – (Windows)

  - A very popular free editor.

Once you have chosen an editor that is right for you, open **index.php** and you can start to write some PHP code to the file. Type in the following code and then save the file:

```
<php echo "Hello World"; ?>
```

Let's run this code. Open up a web browser and, in the browser's address bar, type `http://localhost/my_project/index.php`. You should see something similar to Figure 1.6.

---

[11] http://www.adobe.com/products/dreamweaver.html
[12] http://www.sublimetext.com/
[13] http://www.activestate.com/komodo-edit
[14] http://panic.com/coda/
[15] http://www.notepad-plus-plus.org/

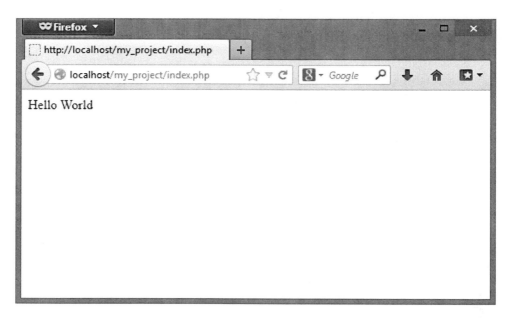

Figure 1.6. Hello, world!

Congratulations! You've just written your first piece of PHP code! As you can see, the code displays the phrase "Hello World" in the web browser, but what exactly have you typed into your PHP file? Let's break down our line of code:

- `<?php` : This is called the opening tag. It tells your server that the code that follows is intended to be interpreted as PHP, and that the server should use the PHP engine to render the code. This tag must be entered every time you want to use PHP code in your file.

- `echo "Hello World";` : `echo` is a basic PHP construct which tells PHP that what follows the `echo` command is something you want to appear in the browser. Quotation marks are added around the text you want to display on screen. Also, you add the important semicolon afterward which signals that your `echo` statement is finished.

- `?>` : This is the closing tag for PHP and tells the server to stop rendering PHP code. The closing tag is not always used. Leaving the code "unclosed" can prevent unintended content from being sent to the browser. Skipping the closing tag when you don't need it can avoid problems which may crop up as you start writing more complex PHP code. Further on in this book you'll see code that doesn't have a closing PHP tag. This tag has been omitted on purpose.

Use Your Semicolons!

It's very important to remember to add a semicolon at the end of all PHP statements because PHP will not know where one statement ends and the next statement begins without it.

PHP files also let you combine PHP code with regular HTML. If you combine PHP and HTML together you can create really nice looking web pages that contain dynamic and complex data, which HTML cannot process and handle on its on.

Here's a quick example of HTML and PHP working together:

```
<!DOCTYPE html>
<head>
    <title>PHP and HTML working together</title>
    </head>
    <body>
      <h1><?php echo 'This is a H1 tag with PHP data'; ?></h1>
      <p><?php echo 'This is a P tag with PHP data also'; ?></p>
    </body>
</html>
```

If you change the contents of the **index.php** file to the example above and navigate back to `http://localhost/my_project/index.php`, you'll see the HTML code display all the code processed by PHP correctly in your browser.

PHP Variables

Let's take our code to the next level and explore the world of variables. A variable represents a place in the computer's memory where we can temporarily store bits of information. We can assign some piece of data to a variable (place the data in memory) and use that variable throughout our script. Each time PHP sees the variable in our code, it knows to access the data that it represents. The data we assign to a variable can be anything from a simple string of text such as "Hello World", or numbers like "1234", through to more complex data structures, which we'll cover shortly.

Variable names are always prefixed with the $ symbol. Their names cannot contain spaces and must only contain letters (lower and upper-case), numbers, and underscores. In addition, the first character in the name after the $ must be a letter or an

underscore. Acceptable variable names could be $myAwesomeVariable, or even
$my_Awesome_Variable_1.

It's considered good practice to give your variables meaningful names so that if another developer reads the code you've written they have a clue as to what data it represents. For example, if we wanted a variable to hold data about someone's name we could call our variable $personName.

 ## Use CamelCase

If your variable has more than one word in its name, it's common practice to give the start of each word a capital letter. This improves readability when scanning through code.

Let's take a look at a variable in use. Modify **index.php** as follows:

```php
<?php
$myVar = 'Hello World, this is using a variable';
echo $myVar;
```

So what have we coded here? First, we assigned a value (the string "Hello World, this is using a variable") to the variable $myVar. As this is the first time we have used the variable $myVar, it is created automatically by PHP. Now if we write $myVar anywhere in the PHP script, PHP will know to load the data we've assigned to that variable.

If you reload the **index.php** file again in your browser, you should see that our string, "Hello World, this is using a variable", is displayed.

Expanding on this code, let's go ahead and change **index.php** file again so it looks like this:

```php
<?php
$myVar;
$myVar = 'Hello World, this is using a variable';
echo $myVar;
$myVar = 'Goodbye World';
echo $myVar;
```

Refresh the page again and you should see both sentences, "Hello World, this is using a variable" and "Goodbye World", appear on the screen. This is because we can overwrite the data in a variable at any time.

The example above also shows how PHP processes and renders our code line-by-line from the top down. Our first `echo` statement shows the first sentence because, at that point, the variable `$myVar` holds that sentence. However, after the first `echo` statement, we overwrite it with our second sentence. It's important to remember the "top-down" rule when you are planning what you want your PHP script to do with certain pieces of data at certain points within your script. If you overwrite a variable's data before you plan to use it, that data will be gone and the script's output will be incorrect.

We can store store more than just strings and sentences in our PHP variables; let's have a quick look at the different types of data we can use:

```php
<?php
$myVar = 0;                          // Integer
$myVar = 3.14;                       // Float
$myVar = "Year to Date";             // String
$myVar = true;                       // Boolean
$myVar = array(250, 300, 325, 475);  // Array
```

In the code above we have used a wide variety of variables types, so let's have a quick run through them:

- Integer – Whole numbers. These can be either positive or negative.

- Float – Numbers with decimal places. These can also be either positive or negative.

- String – A mixture of letters, numbers, and symbols. Strings are surrounded by quotes.

- Boolean – One of two values: `true` or `false`. The value must not have any quotes as this would turn it into a string.

- Array – A multi-level storage type, similar to a table.

For a full run-down of what these types allow us to do in PHP and examples of the amazing things we can do with them, check out a few of these articles and tutorials:

▓ http://www.php.net/manual/en/language.variables.basics.php[16]

▓ http://www.sitepoint.com/variables/[17]

▓ http://goldhat.ca/blog/php-beginner-lesson-using-variables

Arrays

For more complex ways of storing data in memory we have the option of using an array, which represents data just like a table. Let's begin with the table shown in Figure 1.7.

My Array	Item 1 My Value

Figure 1.7. A simple array

We can write this table as an array in PHP like so:

```php
<?php
$myArray = array('item1' => 'My Value');
```

What we've done here is create an array named $myArray by using the array() construct to define our value, rather than just a string or integer. Then we added a "key", which we named "item1" and set the value "My value" to that key by using the => symbol. This => symbol is PHP's way of denoting that the data following the symbol will be stored in a place in memory that can be referenced from the array by that key.

We can add more than one key/data pair to our array when we define it as shown in the following:

```php
<?php
$myArray = array('item1' => 'My Value', 'item2' => 'Another value');
```

---

[16] ???

[17] ???

Another option is that we could've created an empty array and added our key and value later in the following manner:

```php
<?php
$myArray = array();
$myArray['item1'] = 'My Value';
$myArray['item2'] = 'Another value';
```

Since PHP 5.4, we've had the ability to use a shorthand notation for creating an array rather than the traditional `array()`. The shorthand approach looks like this:

```php
<?php
$myArray = ['item1' => 'My Value', 'item2' => 'Another value'];
```

Arrays allow us to work with some very complex data and we'll be returning to them later on in the book. In the meantime, to check out the basic usage of arrays I recommend having a look over following articles:

■ http://www.php.net/manual/en/language.types.array.php

■ http://www.sitepoint.com/introduction-to-php-arrays/

■ http://www.htmlandphp.com/beginner-php/207-introduction-to-arrays-in-php.html

Comments

We can write comments to ourselves in our PHP code. Comments are not processed as statements by PHP. We start a comment by using two forward slashes // — anything written on the same line after the slashes will be considered to be a comment and won't be processed. For example:

```php
<?php
// this is a PHP comment for this line only
```

We can also use /* to signal the beginning of a comment that spans multiple lines ending with */ to mark the end of the comment. For example:

```php
<?php
/* this is the beginning of our PHP comment.
It can go on for multiple lines until we end the comment.
We will end it now. */
```

Comments allow developers to leave notes to anyone reading their code, giving insight into how it works and making it easier to maintain.

Comments also allow us to temporarily hide segments of code ("comment out" code). We might do this with code that isn't yet complete and would cause an error if it was processed.

Preparing Our Project

To conclude this chapter, let's quickly lay out the directory structure for this book's project. We'll be developing a basic blog application powered purely by PHP and a MySQL database to store all our data, such as post content. The application will consist of a public front-end, displaying a list of blog posts, and an admin panel that will enable us to manage our blog's content.

For now, we need to create a new folder in our web directory, which we'll call **kickstart**. Inside this directory we need to make three more directories: one named **admin**, another named **frontend**, and the last one named **includes** as shown in Figure 1.8.

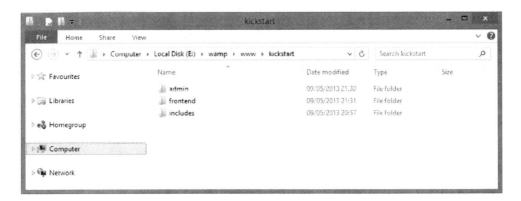

Figure 1.8. Our project folders

The admin directory will house the files used for the admin panel functionality. The **frontend** directory will hold all the files used for the public side of the blog to work. This public side is where visitors will be able to view blog posts, and the files will load the blog data for display in the visitors' browsers. The **includes** directory is where we'll place any scripts which have functionality that can be used in both the admin section and the public section.

We also need to create a directory inside both the **admin** and **frontend** directories named **templates**. The directory templates which will hold all the PHP and HTML files that will accept data from scripts and files in the functions folder. These template files will ultimately format our data from PHP and create the layouts that our visitors will interact with in the front-end. The same template files will also create the layouts which we'll use to manage the blog in the admin section. Further on in the book we'll go into templating in greater depth and learn why exactly we're using it for our project.

Separating out these folders like this is helpful because it'll help you to develop cleaner and better-organized code.

Summary

In this chapter we've covered the basics of setting up a web server, introduced PHP coding by displaying text, and used variables to store PHP data. Everything covered in this chapter is an introduction and we'll be coming back to some of the topics we've touched on here later in the book.

In the next chapter we'll be looking at how we can use permanent storage options such as a database with our scripts and how we can use the visitor's browser to store small amounts of data as well.

2

PHP & Data

Data is the lifeblood of PHP. In this chapter, we'll look at one of the many options
that PHP offers to developers in terms of processing data and using permanent
storage solutions—interacting with a MySQL database. In addition, we'll briefly
explore some important programming concepts, like conditional statements and
loops, which become necessary when reading data back from a database. So get
ready and roll up your sleeves; we're going to dive deep into the world of PHP data
handling!

Operators

In PHP, just as in almost all programming languages, **operators** are used to manipulate or perform various operations on variables and values. The most basic operator
is =, which as we saw in Chapter 1 is used to assign a value to a variable. But there
are many other powerful operators to discover.

To begin, let's create a new file named **op_experiments.php** in the **my_project** folder
that we created previously. In this file, add the following code:

```php
<?php
$firstName = "myfirstname";
$lastName = "mylastname";
$fullName = $firstName . $lastName;
echo $fullName;
```

While most of this code probably looks pretty straightforward, the line $fullName = $firstName . $lastName; may take you slightly by surprise, especially the little period that sits between two of the variables.

The period is PHP's string concatenation operator; it joins two strings together to make one longer string. PHP takes the string value of $firstName, adds the value of $lastName to it, and places the result in the variable $fullName. When we run the script and PHP outputs the value of $fullName, we will see myfirstnamemylastname displayed in the browser.

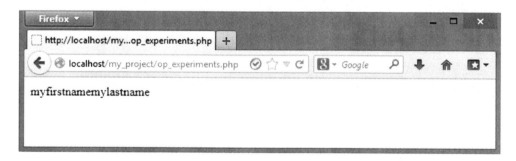

Figure 2.1. The output of our experiment

It's not very readable though, is it? No worries. We can easily tweak the code a little to make the output more readable. Modify the code so it looks like the following:

```php
<?php
$firstName = "myfirstname";
$lastName = "mylastname";
$fullName = $firstName . " - " . $lastName;
echo $fullName;
```

Now we can see the separation between our two names when we view them in the browser. Cool.

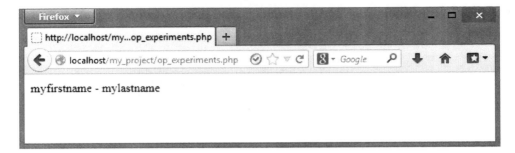

Figure 2.2. The output after adding some spaces

Conditional Statements

PHP also has operators that allow us to compare values. For example == checks to see if two values are the same, < if a value is less than another, and > if a value is greater than another.

Most of the time we use these comparison operators to write **conditional statements** (statements that may or may not execute depending on the result of a comparison) and **loops** (statements that execute multiple times over).

if Statement

An if statement consists of a condition and one or more statements grouped as a block. If PHP evaluates the condition and finds it to be true, then it will execute the block of statements. If the condition is false, then PHP will skip the block. In the example below, PHP checks to see if the value of $a is equal to $b. If so, it displays "A is equal to B" on the screen:

```php
<?php
if ($a == $b) {
    echo 'A is equal to B';
}
```

else Statement

A partner to the if statement, an else statement can directly follow an if statement. PHP executes the code that makes up the else's block only if it skipped that of the if statement. In the example below, PHP checks to see if the value of $a is equal to $b. If so, it displays "A is equal to B" on the screen: If that test fails, PHP executes the code in the block after the else statement and prints "A is not equal to B" to the screen.

```php
<?php
if ($a == $b) {
    echo 'A is equal to B';
} else {
    echo 'A is not equal to B';
}
```

elseif Statement

Another partner is the `elseif` statement. As its name suggests, `elseif` is a combination of `if` and `else`. It has a condition, and PHP checks the condition if the `if` condition was found to be false.

Multiple `elseif` statements can be used together to test for different conditions, and PHP checks each one until one of the conditions is found to be true. Once a true condition is found, PHP will skip the rest of the `elseif` statements in the chain.

```php
<?php
if ($a == $b) {
    echo 'A is equal to B';
} elseif ($a == $c) {
    echo 'A is equal to C';
} elseif ($a == $d) {
    echo 'A is equal to D';
} else {
    echo 'A is not equal to anything';
}
```

switch Statement

If you take a closer look at our `elseif` example you may notice that each condition basically tests for the same thing—whether the value of some variable is equal to the value of $a. PHP's `switch` statement can do something similar, and also looks a bit less cluttered.

```php
switch ($a) {
    case $b:
        echo 'A equals B';
```

```
        break;
    case $c:
        echo 'A equals C';
        break;
    case $d:
        echo 'A equals D';
        break;
    default:
        echo 'A is not equal to anything';
        break;
}
```

In the example above, PHP takes the value provided at the start of the switch (the value of $a) and compares it to the value of each case. The matching clause is the one that is executed. The default case is executed if none of the other cases match.

Once PHP finds a matching clause, it starts executing the code below and continues until it sees the break keyword, after which it will jump to the end of the switch statement and merrily continue on executing the rest of our script.

 Watch for the Break

PHP doesn't see the start of one case as the end of the previous case, which is why the break keyword is necessary. This might be confusing at first, and there will be likely be times that you forget to use break and your scripts don't do what you intend, so it's important to keep this in mind.

This behavior also means that we can write code that executes for multiple cases, like so:

```
switch ($a) {
    case $b:
    case $c:
    case $d:
        echo 'A equals B, C, or D';
        break;
```

```
        default:
            echo 'A is not equal to anything';
    }
```

Conditional statements give us the ability to write dynamic scripts that execute differently according to different circumstances. I encourage you to practice writing some conditional statements of your own, and to read the official PHP documentation[1].

Loops

Loops in PHP allow us to write one set of statements and have them execute multiple times over. For example, suppose we want to display all of the numbers counting from 1 to 100. Of course we could write 100 lines of code, each using echo to output a different number, but a better way would be to write a loop that repeatedly executes a single echo statement but with a number that increments each time until all 100 numbers are displayed.

for Loop

The for loop is a generic looping mechanism that uses a variable to keep track of its progress and has four main parts: variable initialization (setting a tracking variable or counter to a known starting value), condition (PHP will continue to execute the loop as long as this condition holds true), an increment or decrement (adjusting the value of the counter to mark the progress of the loop), and a block of statements to repeat over.

While that might seem complex and lengthy, it's really quite succinct in code, as this example shows:

```
for ($i = 1; $i < 101; $i = $i + 1) {
    echo $i . '<br>';
}
```

So how does PHP execute this code? Well, it starts by setting the variable $i with the value of 1. Then it looks at the condition and determines that 1 is indeed less

---

[1] http://www.php.net/manual/en/language.control-structures.php

than 101 and executes the loop's block. The block only has one statement in our example, echo which outputs "1" followed by an HTML line break tag. After it executes all of the statements in the block, PHP goes back up to the start of the for loop to execute the third part, $i = $i + 1. This has the effect of updating our tracking variable to 2. Again the condition is checked, 2 is less than 101, and the block is executed. This time around, echo outputs the value "2". PHP keeps repeating the loop until $i reaches 101 (which makes the condition false because the value of $i is then equal to, not less than, 101) and then breaks out of the loop.

while Loop

while loops work in an almost identical fashion to for loops, with the exception being that they only require the condition at their start. It's our responsibility as programmers to set the initial value of our tracking variable before the start of the loop and then adjust it within the loop's statements.

```php
$i = 1;
while ($i < 101){
    echo $i . '<br>';
    $i = $i + 1;
}
```

PHP first sets $i to 1 in our first statement, and then starts the while loop as our second. It checks the condition (which is true) and continues to execute the two statements that make up the loop's body; the value of $i is outputted and then increased in preparation for the next round of execution.

 Have an Escape Plan

An all-too-common mistake when working with loops is to forget to adjust the counter. If the value never changes then the condition will always stay true; the loop will never stop repeating! When you write a loop, always make sure that you've a way for it to stop at some point.

foreach

Where the for and while loops made use of an explicit condition, PHP's foreach loop operates in a different way. It takes a multi-key variable (an array for example) and executes a set of statements for each element.

```
$myArray = array('Hello', 'World');
foreach ($myArray as $value) {
    echo $value . '<br>';
}
```

For each member in the array $myArray, PHP assigns its value to the $value variable making it available to statements that make up the loop's body.

There's a second variation on the foreach loop that's handy to know. We can also access the key of the current element along with the value if we write it like so:

```
$myArray = array(1 => 'Hello', 2 => 'World');
foreach ($myArray as $key => $value) {
    echo $key . ': ' . $value . '<br>';
}
```

For more information on while, for, and foreach loops, please see the PHP official documentation[2] as well as the resources below:

- http://www.sitepoint.com/loops/

- http://webcheatsheet.com/PHP/loops.php

Databases, MySQL, and PHP

When we create a PHP web application, more often than not we require some of the data created in our script to be saved somewhere for future access. A database allows us to store large amounts of different types of data, from large alphanumeric strings to serialized arrays. MySQL is the most popular open source database available, and it works incredibly well with PHP to store our application's data. It's very easy to get up and running and only requires a few functions to store and retrieve data.

Traditional databases like MySQL use tables, rows, and columns to organize data. Each table holds a set of records (user information, order summaries, etc.), each row in a table stores a specific record, and each column identifies a different piece of data that makes up the record. A database table can be envisioned like Figure 2.3.

---

[2] http://www.php.net/manual/en/language.control-structures.php

Row 1 Column 1	Row 1 Column 2	Row 1 Column 3
Row 2 Column 1	Row 2 Column 2	Row 2 Column 3
Row 3 Column 1	Row 3 Column 2	Row 3 Column 3

Figure 2.3. A database table

Think About Data Types

Since each column in a table is only allowed to store one type of data, and this is often part of the column's definition, it's important to think about the different properties of the data that you'll be storing beforehand.

Before continuing, it's important that you're familiar yourself with the purpose of databases and the basics of MySQL. If you're unsure about any of that, please read the MySQL article on tizag.com[3].http://www.tizag.com/mysqlTutorial

There are two extensions for working with MySQL in PHP—MySQLi and PDO. We're going to use the PDO extension to connect to and interact with our MySQL database, so make sure the extension is installed and enabled. Open the file **info.php** we wrote in Chapter 1, look for the section titled **PDO**, and make sure that MySQL is listed in the **enabled** column.

Problems Installing PDO

If you have problems enabling the extension, check out the PHP Manual's guide to installing PDO[4].

The highly popular phpMyAdmin is a PHP application that makes managing multiple databases a breeze. With this in mind, it's highly recommended that you make sure that phpMyAdmin is installed on your server. We'll be using it to manage our database throughout this book.

---

[3] http://www.tizag.com/mysqlTutorial
[4] http://php.net/manual/en/pdo.installation.php

To get started, we need to create a new empty database using phpMyAdmin. To do this, open your installation of phpMyAdmin in your browser and log in. You should be welcomed with a screen similar to the following:

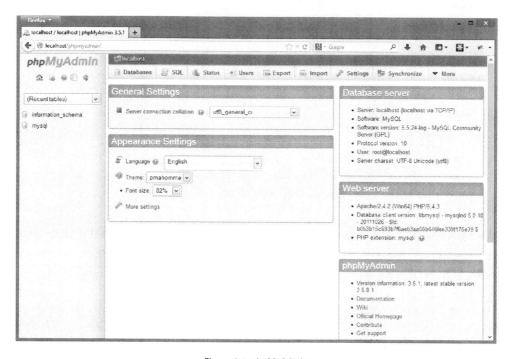

Figure 2.4. phpMyAdmin

Next, click on the **Databases** link in the top menu. In the next screen we can create our new database by typing the name of the database we want to use. For our project, let's type "kickstartapp" into the text field and hit the create button.

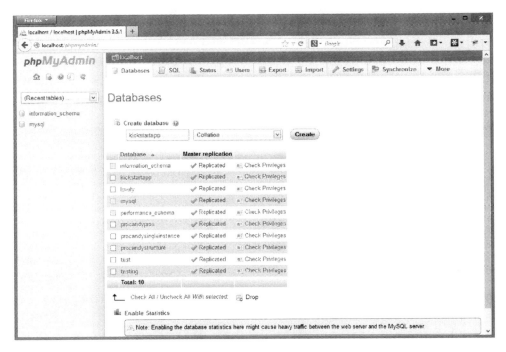

Figure 2.5. Creating our databases

 ## Collation?

Don't worry about the drop-down option which should be preselected to "Collation". This is a more advanced feature and, for the purposes of the book's project, we'll be sticking to the default options. If you'd like to read up about database collation types, please see:

- http://dev.mysql.com/doc/refman/5.0/en/charset-collation-implementations.html

- https://kb.mediatemple.net/questions/138/Default+MySQL+character+set+and+collation#gs

 ## Take Care When Naming your Databases

When we create a database, its name cannot contain slashes, periods, or other characters that are not permitted in file names, and should not contain spaces.

Those with a keen eye may have noticed that our newly created database has been added to the list of accessible databases. This list on the left-hand menu is a collection of quick links that we can use to select which database we want to edit or manage. Find the new database "kickstartapp" in the list and click on it. This will take us to a new screen which will look fairly empty and similar to Figure 2.6:

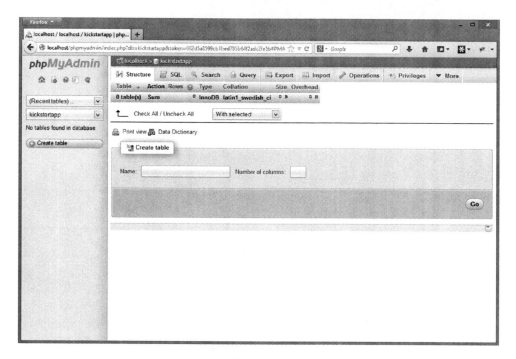

Figure 2.6. Our new database

This is the main area of phpMyAdmin where we can create tables and edit existing ones for our database. But before we do this, we need to create a user account which will be used to connect to the database and store and extract our data.

Head to the **Privileges** option in the top menu and click on it, then, in the new panel, select **Add User**, as shown in Figure 2.7.

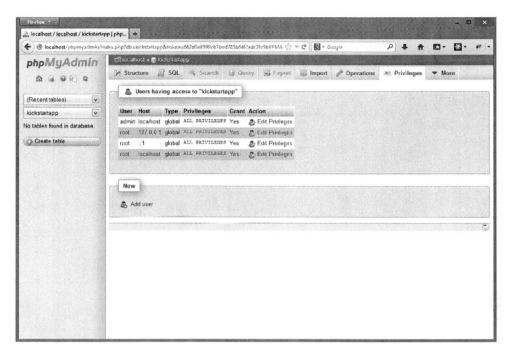

Figure 2.7. Adding a new user

Now we just need to enter a user name into the field **User name** (make sure **use text field** is also selected from the drop-down menu), select **local** in the **Host** drop-down and then enter a password into the password fields (again making sure **use text field** is selected). Next, scroll down and make sure **Grant all privileges on database kickstartapp** is checked in the next option area in the panel. Finally, select **Check all** under **Global privileges** in the final panel and hit **Add User** at the bottom of the panel.

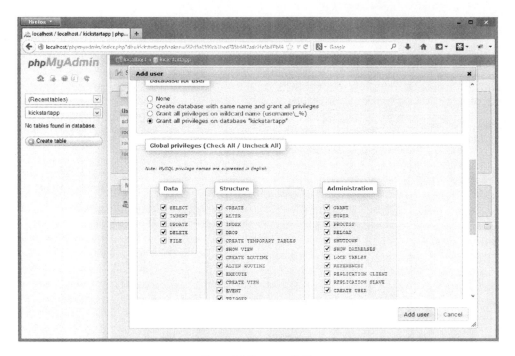

Figure 2.8. New user fields

That might seem a bit complex, but actually all we did was create a new user and then give that user the right to do anything to the database "kickstartapp". This setup is the most common for users of databases, but not necessarily the most secure. You can change the user privileges to be more restrictive if you like. For more information on setting up database users, please see:

- http://dev.mysql.com/doc/refman/5.1/en/adding-users.html

- https://kb.mediatemple.net/questions/788/HOWTO%3A+GRANT+priv-ileges+in+MySQL#dv

Now that we have a user account set up, let's create a table in our database. Create a new PHP script in our project folder named **setup.php**. In this file, add the following code and then save and run the file through the browser.

Customize Your Code

Replace the text **USERNAME** and **PASSWORD** in the following code with the username and password you set when you created your user for the database.

```php
<?php
$db = new PDO("mysql:host=localhost;dbname=kickstartapp",
➥ "USERNAME", "PASSWORD");
$db->setAttribute(PDO::ATTR_ERRMODE, PDO::ERRMODE_EXCEPTION);
try {
    $queryStr = "CREATE TABLE users (id INTEGER NOT NULL
➥AUTO_INCREMENT PRIMARY KEY, name VARCHAR(40), password
➥VARCHAR(100), email VARCHAR(150))";
    $db->query($queryStr);
} catch (PDOException $e) {
    echo $e->getMessage();
}
```

First we connect to MySQL on from PHP by creating a PDO object with four key pieces of information. The first tells PHP where our MySQL database is located. In our case, this is "localhost" as the MySQL server is running on the same system that PHP is running on. The second identifies which database we want to connect to. Together, these two bits of information are combined with mysql: to create what is called a **DSN**, or Data Source Name. The third and fourth arguments are simply the username and password for the database user we created.

Next we set a feedback option for PDO that causes any database errors to be treated as exceptions by PHP. With this, if anything goes wrong when MySQL tries to execute the SQL we provide, we'll be alerted immediately, and will be able to see what happened so we can fix it.

Then we define the SQL statement that will create the table and assign the string to the variable $queryStr. Looking at the SQL, we're telling MySQL to create a new table named users which we'll use to store all of the data related to both admin users and public users for our blogging application. This is done with the CREATE TABLE command followed by the definitions for the different columns we want in our table: id, name, password, and email. Each column definition tells MySQL what type of data the column will hold as well as any other options for that cell. For example, the first column (id) will hold only integer numbers and a record will never be allowed to have an empty value for it (NOT NULL).

Next we have a type of conditional statement that we haven't discussed yet: a try...catch block. In the try block, we pass the $queryStr variable to the query() method of the PDO object. The method takes our SQL string and sends it to the MySQL server to be executed.

PHP executes code in a `catch` block only if there was a problem in the `try` block. That is, PHP will "throw" an exception if MySQL fails to run our query (we asked for this behavior by setting `PDO::ATTR_ERRMODE` earlier). Our `catch` block will "catch" the exception object which has information we can use to troubleshoot the problem.

Go ahead and access **setup.php** file through your browser. If the screen remains blank, the query executed successfully (we only asked PHP to output anything if there was a problem). Then head back to phpMyAdmin and click on the database to verify that the newly created table exists.

Now let's add some data to our table! Create a new file in the project directory named **insert.php** and add the following code to it:

```php
<?php
$db = new PDO("mysql:host=localhost;dbname=kickstartapp",
➥ "USERNAME", "PASSWORD");
$db->setAttribute(PDO::ATTR_ERRMODE, PDO::ERRMODE_EXCEPTION);
try {
    $queryStr = "INSERT INTO users (username, password, email)
➥VALUES ('admin', MD5('admin'), 'youremail@domain.com')";
    $db->query($queryStr);
} catch (PDOException $e) {
    echo $e->getMessage();
}
```

Much of the code is the same as before, except the SQL we're sending to MySQL is now an `INSERT INTO` command. We're asking MySQL to create a new record in the `users` table with the username "admin", a password hash, and an email address.

Using MD5

Notice that for the `password` column we used the `MD5()` function to hash the data. This is done for security reasons so that anyone who gains unauthorized access to our database cannot easily view our users' passwords. Never store passwords in plain text!

Navigate to the **insert.php** file and you should again hopefully see a blank page meaning the query has executed successfully, otherwise you will see a error message giving insight into what went wrong. Head back to phpMyAdmin and look inside the users table inside the kickstartapp database by clicking on the table's name. You should see that the data has been inserted into the table.

Finally, let's retrieve data from the table in a different PHP script. Create the file **getdata.php** and add the following code:

```php
<?php
$db = new PDO("mysql:host=localhost;dbname=kickstartapp",
➥ "USERNAME", "PASSWORD");
$db->setAttribute(PDO::ATTR_ERRMODE, PDO::ERRMODE_EXCEPTION);
try {
    $queryStr = "SELECT * FROM users";
    $query = $db->prepare($queryStr);
    $query->execute();
    while ($row = $query->fetch()) {
        echo $row['id'] . ' - ' . $row['name'] . ' - ' .
➥$row['email'] . ' - ' . $row['password'];
        echo '<br>';
    }
    $query->closeCursor();
} catch (PDOException $e) {
    echo $e->getMessage();
}
```

Again, a lot of this code should look familiar, but this time we're sending a SELECT command to MySQL, which means we'll be receiving data back from the database. The command, as we've written it, selects all columns of all of the rows in the users table.

The prepare() method prepares the query to be sent to the database and returns a statement object which we assign to the variable $query. This statement object has methods which we can use to access the records that are returned by MySQL. Then the execute() method tells PDO to send the query to MySQL, and we're off and running.

The statement object's fetch() method returns one record from the database as an array each time it's called (each of the columns become a member in the array, and the column names are used as keys to access the data). When there are no more records to return, fetch() returns a Boolean false.

Each time the `while` loop is executed, we assign the database record that was returned from `fetch()` to the variable `$row`, and the result of the assignment is used as the loop's condition. When a record is returned, PHP considers that a true condition and executes the loop's statements. When `fetch()` returns false because there are no more records to process, PHP considers that a false condition and stops repeating the loop.

Finally, we call the `closeCursor()` method which clears out the connection we had between PHP and MySQL for the query and frees the memory used by PHP to receive the result set. This method isn't always required, but it's good practice and I highly recommend using it every time you finish receiving data from a query with PDO.

If we take to our browser and navigate to **getdata.php** we should see all of the data that's in the `users` table. If there is an error in either the PHP code or in the SQL sent to MySQL, you'll see a message which should give you some hint as to how to fix the issue.

Summary

In this chapter we've covered the basics of creating a database using phpMyAdmin, creating a table in PHP using MySQL commands, inserting a record, and retrieving rows of data from a table. However, this is only the tip of the iceberg. Both MySQL and PHP go so much deeper than what we've seen here. For more information on MySQL and using MySQL with PHP, please see the following resources:

- http://dev.mysql.com/doc/

- http://www.sitepoint.com/migrate-from-the-mysql-extension-to-pdo/

- http://www.php.net/manual/en/book.pdo.php

- http://www.sitepoint.com/avoid-the-original-mysql-extension-1/

Objects and OOP

In this book, we'll be using the **Object Oriented Programming** (OOP) paradigm. With OOP, we can create "objects" that combine data and the functions that operate on that data together. Because objects in OOP collect data and the functions that work on them in one place, we keep our code organized and can better manage complexity as our application grows.

The code that we write to define an object is called a **class**. One way to better understand the relationship between classes and objects is to think of a home builder. The builder—PHP for our purposes—follows a blueprint (a class) to build a house (an object).

Just as a builder can construct several houses using the same blueprint, so too can PHP create multiple instances of an object. Each house has the same layout, but may be painted differently and obviously will have different families living in it. In PHP, each object created from the same class has the same functionality, but its properties and data that "live" inside the object are unique to that instance.

OOP may seem complex at first glance, but it's actually a very straightforward approach to programming. For more information about the theory behind OOP, please see Lorna Mitchell's video introduction to OOP in PHP on sitepoint.com.[1]

First Steps in OOP

Let's write a small OOP example together. Suppose we want to represent a dog as an object in our PHP code. We'll need to write the definition for the object (class) that describes what the dog can do.

Create a new file named **Dog.php** in your **experiments** folder with the following content:

```php
<?php
class Dog
{
    public $name;

    public function __construct($name) {
        $this->name = $name;
    }

    public function speak() {
        return 'Woof! Woof!';
    }
}
```

Let's create another file in the **experiments** folder, **DogTest.php**.

```php
<?php
require 'Dog.php';

$dog = new Dog('Fido');
echo 'The dog\'s name is: ' . $dog->name . '<br>';
echo 'The dog says: ' . $dog->speak() . '<br>';
```

Navigate to the **DogTest.php** file in your browser and you should see the dog's name and barking on your screen. Great stuff.

---

[1] http://www.sitepoint.com/object-oriented-php-lesson-1/

Including Code From Other Files

The `require` construct seen in the example above—in a nutshell—imports the contents of an external PHP file into our **DogTest.php** file. It's one of four such constructs used to include code from other files, each with slightly different behavior:

- `include` — includes the contents of the file. If the file isn't found or is inaccessible, PHP will issue a warning but will continue executing.

- `include_once` — the same as `include`, but PHP performs an extra check to make sure the file hasn't been imported already. If it has, then PHP will not re-include the contents.

- `require` — similar to `include` but PHP will stop execution with a fatal error if the file isn't found.

- `require_once` — the same as `require` but with an extra check to ensure the content isn't imported more than once.

Taking a look at our **Dog.php** file, the first thing we notice is the `class` keyword. This keyword basically states that the following code defines a class that will be known by the name that follows it (in our case, `Dog`). Once the class is defined, we can create an object from it using `new Dog`.

The methods `__construct()` and `speak()` are part of the class definition. `__construct` is a name that has special meaning to PHP; when we create a new object from the class, PHP looks to see if a `__construct()` method is defined. If so, it will automatically execute this method after it creates an instance of the object. This makes it a great place to put any code that is responsible for initializing a new object.

Functions and Methods

Functions that belong to a class are called **methods**. There's little difference between a function and a method, so it's safe to imagine the word "function" every time you see "method" if it helps your understanding.

A class can have its own set of variables that help the object instance maintain its state, and which are accessible to its methods. The line `public $name;` in our **Dog.php** example above defines `$name` as a class variable, or property.

Variables and Properties

Variables that belong to a class are called **properties**. Like functions/methods, it's safe to imagine the word "variable" every time you see "property" until you become comfortable with OOP terminology.

When we're writing code inside a class, the special variable $this represents the instance of the object, and helps us to resolve a method or property correctly. To better understand how this works, let's update the **DogTest.php** file so it looks like this:

```php
<?php
  require 'Dog.php';

  $fido = new Dog('Fido');
  echo 'The dog\'s name is: ' . $fido->name . '<br>';
  echo 'The dog says: ' . $fido->speak() . '<br>';

  $fifi = new Dog('Fifi');
  echo 'The dog\'s name is: ' . $fifi->name . '<br>';
  echo 'The dog says: ' . $fifi->speak() . '<br>';
```

We've changed the variable $dog to be named $fido instead, and created another instance of a Dog object with the name "Fifi". When you run the code, you should see both Fido and Fifi barking on your screen. But let's think about what's happening behind the scenes here to make this work.

Each object is of the same class (Dog), but each is its own distinct instance with its own data—for example, each has its own $name property. When the $fido instance is created, the name "Fido" is assigned to it's $name variable, whereas the name "Fifi" is assigned as the name of the $fifi instance.

Watch the Arrows

When calling a method or property, you need to remember to use the -> operator. This lets PHP know you're referencing something that specifically belongs to the class instead of a regular variable or function in the execution scope of the script. Keep this in mind when calling methods or variables because calling the wrong thing can cause unpredictable results in your PHP scripts!

Extending Classes

Now you have a very basic understanding of OOP, so let's recap briefly. A class is a definition that groups variables and functions together into a logical unit, and a specific instance in memory that was created based on the class is called an object. Obviously, though, there's more to OOP than just this. Another important aspect is the ability to **extend** a class in order to add or improve functionality without having to re-code the aspects of it that stay the same.

To understand **inheritance**—creating a new class by extending an existing class—let's create the **Pet.php** file with the definition of a **Pet** class. This will serve as a **base class**, which we will then extend with other classes to make specific types of pets, such as a dog, cat, fish, lizard, etc.

```php
<?php
class Pet
{
    public $name;

    public function __construct($name) {
        $this->name = $name;
    }

    public function speak() {
        return 'nothing';
    }
}
```

This class is intentionally very similar to our **Dog** class, so there shouldn't be anything too surprising here. Now let's re-write the **Dog** class so that it extends **Pet** and reuses its functionality.

```php
<?php
require_once 'Pet.php';

class Dog extends Pet
{
    public function speak() {
        return 'Woof! Woof!';
    }
}
```

```php
    public function plays() {
        return 'fetch';
    }
}
```

And just for fun, let's create a few more animal classes. Create the file `Cat.php`:

```php
<?php
require_once 'Pet.php';

class Cat extends Pet
{
    public function speak() {
        return 'Meow!';
    }

    public function plays() {
        return 'chase mice';
    }
}
```

... and the file `Fish.php`:

```php
<?php
require_once 'Pet.php';

class Fish extends Pet
{
}
```

Now let's test them out. Create the file **PetTest.php** with the following code:

```php
<?php
require 'Dog.php';
require 'Cat.php';
require 'Fish.php';

$fido = new Dog('Fido');
echo 'The dog\'s name is: ' . $fido->name . '<br>';
echo 'The dog says: ' . $fido->speak() . '<br>';
echo 'The dog plays: ' . $fido->plays() . '<br>';

$mittens = new Cat('Mittens');
```

```
echo 'The cat\'s name is: ' . $mittens->name . '<br>';
echo 'The cat says: ' . $mittens->speak() . '<br>';
echo 'The cat plays: ' . $mittens->plays() . '<br>';

$bubbles = new Fish('Bubbles');
echo 'The fish\'s name is: ' . $bubbles->name . '<br>';
echo 'The fish says: ' . $bubbles->speak() . '<br>';
```

Now things are starting to get interesting! Go ahead and create classes that define a Parrot class and a Lizard class, and update **PetTest.php** to create an instance of each, display their names, and what they might say.

When we extend a class, we are basically building one class from another. This creates a parent/child relationship. For example, we can say the Dog class is a child of Pet, and Pet is a parent of Dog. By building on previously written code, we don't have to repeat ourselves by writing the same code elsewhere and, as a result, we'll have better organized, more efficient code.

Each class that represent a specific type of pets inherit the methods and properties from the parent Pet class. Consider the Fish class... it has no code of its own and inherits all of its behavior from Pet.

The Dog and Cat classes, on the other hand, extend the Pet class but also override the speak() methods with their own version and add new functionality with plays() methods.

 ## What's With Public?

In classes, we attach what is called a **visibility** to our objects and our methods. We always have three choices when assigning: **public, protected** or **private**. Public means the class's objects and methods can be accessed by calls from anywhere. Protected means the objects and methods can only be accessed by methods and calls which are in the same class tree as the method or object being called. Private means the methods and objects can only be accessed by the class that the method or object belongs to.

For more information on visibility in classes, please check out the following resources:

      ▪ php.net/manual/en/language.oop5.visibility.php[2]

      ▪ aperiplus.sourceforge.net/visibility.php[3]

      ▪ www.sitepoint.com/learn-object-oriented-php/[4]

We've covered the very basics of using OOP in PHP above. While it can seem like a very complex and sophisticated coding strategy at first, it's actually more like riding a bike; once you learn it, you'll never forget it.

OOP not only helps makes developing large and complex applications easier, but it's also an approach that appears in almost every other professional programming language. Learning and mastering it in PHP can help you understand other programming languages in the future, so it's an incredibly useful skill to have.

From here on in, we'll assume that you're comfortable with OOP and the use of classes and objects in PHP. To aid your understanding of the topics we discussed, it's recommended that you check out these links:

▪ http://codular.com/introducing-php-classes

▪ http://www.php5-tutorial.com/classes/introduction/

▪ http://php.net/manual/en/keyword.extends.php

▪ http://jadendreamer.wordpress.com/2011/05/13/php-tutorial-learning-oop-class-basics-extending-classes/

▪ http://www.killerphp.com/tutorials/object-oriented-php/

▪ http://www.techotopia.com/index.php/PHP_Object_Oriented_Programming

▪ http://www.techflirt.com/tutorials/oop-in-php/index.html

▪ http://net.tutsplus.com/tutorials/php/object-oriented-php-for-beginners/

---

[2] http://php.net/manual/en/language.oop5.visibility.php
[3] http://aperiplus.sourceforge.net/visibility.php
[4] http://www.sitepoint.com/learn-object-oriented-php/

Templates

As we discussed in the first chapter, PHP files can handle both PHP code and HTML, which makes it ideal for introducing new coders who have experience with HTML to the world of server-side development. But when you start building and complex applications, mixing PHP and HTML code together can cause confusion. And in larger development teams, there may be team members who specialize in front-end development and those who specialize in back-end development. Mixing front-end code with back-end code in such environments can cause complications as team members try not to get in each others' way.

Templating allows us to separate our front-end display logic from the data crunching processes that run on the back-end. There are a few programming patterns built around OOP that encourage templating, the most famous being the MVC (Model-View-Controller) architecture pattern, which appears in several well-known frameworks, such as CakePHP[5], Zend Framework[6], and CodeIgniter[7]. The MVC pattern separates code into different areas of concern allowing us to better organize our code base.

There are a few types of templating we can perform, but the simplest relies on loading a PHP file that's mainly made up of HTML code. The purpose of any snippet of PHP that may be interspersed around the file is only to display the content of a variable. We set the variable elsewhere in a PHP-only file, and then include the template for it to manage the display. Let's look at an example.

First, the template file would look like this:

```
<?php
<html>
 <head>
  <title><?php echo $pageTitle; ?></title>
 </head>
 <body>
  <ul>
<?php foreach ($array as $item) {?>
   <li><?php echo $item; ?></li>
```

---

[5] http://cakephp.org/
[6] http://framework.zend.com/
[7] http://ellislab.com/codeigniter

```
<?php } ?>
  </ul>
 </body>
</html>
```

Then, a PHP script would set the variables and include the template, like so:

```
<?php
$pageTitle = 'My Template Example';
$array = array('one', 'two', 'three');
require 'path/to/template.php';
```

When the template is included, it inherits the scope of the calling file and has access to all the variables, functions, classes, etc. that the calling file possesses.

The advantages of using this method of templating are:

- It's simple to implement. It doesn't require a special third-party template-rendering library to be available to your application.

- Templates can still process PHP. The template can still loop through arrays, call functions, etc.

However, there are also some negatives to using this approach:

- Front-end developers using the templates must know PHP. Any developers working with the templates must know PHP and how to develop in it.

- It's not true templating. Strictly speaking, these "templates" are not actually templates because they're just extra PHP files used to dictate the layout of the data within the application.

An alternative to is to use special templating libraries that offer their own syntax. They're very different from the templates we just discussed because, in order to render the template with data, you don't use any PHP. Instead, you use special syntax unique to the library that usually looks like a cross between PHP and plain text. When the library renders the template, the library replaces the special syntax with the data that it represents.

One famous example of templating that takes this approach can be found in Expression Engine CMS[8], where all the templates contain specific code blocks to display various bits of data.

```php
<?php
<html>
 <head>
  <title>{% pageTitle %}</title>
 </head>
 <body>
  <ul>
{% if array as element %}
   <li>{% element %}</li>
{% /if %}
  </ul>
 </body>
</html>
```

Advantages to using this method of templating are:

- There's no need to learn PHP. Front-end developers using the templates can be given a list of code blocks to use for requesting data from PHP, therefore removing the need to learn PHP coding and its syntax.

- It uses standard HTML files. The template files can retain their traditional HTML file extension.

However, there are some disadvantages to using this templating approach as well:

- A rendering library is required. You'll need to have a third-party library to process the templates available to your application.

- Each library may have its own special syntax and functionality. This can effect your application's processing structure or may conflict with your own personal style of coding.

Both approaches clearly have their pros and cons, and it's worthwhile becoming familiar with the various templating options to see what works best for your applic-

---

[8] http://ellislab.com/expressionengine

ation. For more information on templating, it's recommended that you check out the following resources:

- http://www.broculos.net/2008/03/how-to-make-simple-html-template-engine.html

- http://coding.smashingmagazine.com/2011/10/17/getting-started-with-php-templating/

- http://www.sitepoint.com/smarty-php-template-engine/

- http://www.sitepoint.com/beyond-template-engine/

Project Files

Now that we've had a look at OOP and templating, it's time that we start implementing these powerful coding practices in our blogging application, allowing us to build the framework of our app. We'll need to add a number of files; Figure 3.1 shows you what the root directory should look like, Figure 3.2 shows the **admin** directory, Figure 3.3 shows the **includes** directory, and Figure 3.4 shows the **frontend** directory.

Figure 3.1. Main directory

Figure 3.2. Admin directory

Figure 3.3. Includes directory

Figure 3.4. Frontend directory

We'll just add some skeleton code to outline how they're going to function. In each of the files listed, add the code that follows. Once it's added, be sure to save the file.

index.php

```php
<?php
require_once('includes/posts.php');

$blog = new Posts;

$admin = new Comments;
```

login.php

```php
<?php
    require_once('includes/login.php');

    $login = new Login;
```

```php
<?php

class Database{

    public $dbserver = '';
    public $username = '';
    public $password = '';
    public $database = '';
    public $db = '';

    public function __construct(){
        $this->dbserver = 'localhost';
        $this->username = 'xxx';
        $this->password = 'xxx';
        $this->database = 'xxx';
        $this->db = new PDO("mysql:host=".$this->dbserver.";
dbname=".$this->database, $this->username, $this->password);
    }

    public function dbselect($table, $select, $where=NULL){

    }

    public function dbadd($tablename, $insert, $format){

    }

    public function dbupdate($tablename, $insert, $where){

    }

}
```

```php
<?php
    session_start();
    require_once('database.php');
    class Adminpanel{
        public function __construct(){
        }
    }
```

```php
class Posts extends Adminpanel{

    public function __construct(){
        parent::__construct();
    }

    public function listPosts(){

    }

    public function editPosts(){

    }

    public function addPost(){
    }

    public function savePost(){


    }

    public function deletePost(){

    }

}

class Comments extends Adminpanel{

    public function __construct(){
        parent::__construct();
    }

    public function listComments(){

    }

    public function deletePost(){

    }

}

$admin = new Adminpanel();
```

includes/login.php

```php
<?php
    require_once('database.php');
    class Login{

        public function __construct(){

        }

        public function index(){

        }

        public function loginSuccess(){

        }

        public function loginFail(){

        }

        private function validateDetails(){

        }

    }
```

includes/posts.php

```php
?php

require_once('database.php');

class Blog{
    public $ksdb = '';
    public $base = '';
    public function __construct(){
        $this->ksdb = new Database;
        $this->base = new stdClass;
        $this->base->url = "http://".$_SERVER['SERVER_NAME'];

    }
}
```

```php
class Posts extends Blog{

    public function __construct(){
        parent::__construct();
    }

    public function getPosts(){

    }

    public function viewPost($postId){

    }
}

class Comments extends Blog{

    public function __construct(){
        parent::__construct();
    }

    public function commentNumber($postId){

    }

    public function getComments($postId){

    }

    public function addComment(){

    }

}
```

Now, that may seem like a lot to take in, but don't worry. In the next chapter we'll be going over each of the files and their functions in detail as we build the functionality that makes the real guts of the application.

Summary

In this chapter we've seen two practices that help us keep our code organized and manageable: OOP and templating.

OOP allows developers to write code that is organized and reusable. You'll find OOP patterns in almost every computer programming language, so learning and mastering OOP will improve your knowledge and skills as a developer.

Templating is another pattern that can keep our code well organized and helps prevent front-end developers and back-end developers from getting in each other's way.

In the next chapter we'll go over each of the files we created for our blogging application and discuss their methods in detail as we build up the functionality for the core of our application.

Chapter

4

Forms

Forms are a vital part of any web application; they're commonly used as a way for visitors to provide information to websites. If you've done any type of HTML or web development, the chances are you've spent at least a little time with forms—perhaps connecting them to a third-party system for validation or processing. PHP can work with very complex forms to enable users to submit data to be validated and processed by your application.

In this chapter we're going to look at the various ways PHP can collect the data submitted from a form, and discuss how to validate it, preparing it for entry into our MySQL database. Later on, we'll carry on building our blog platform and will add a working admin panel.

Form Elements

To start with, let's go over the basic elements that make up a working HTML form. Forms are built with various HTML tags, such as `<form>`, `<input>`, `<textarea>`, `<select>`, and `<optgroup>`, for handling data input. There are also `<label>` tags for labeling inputs, although the data attached to these labels isn't passed through the form when it's submitted.

The foundation of the form is an important part of how the data is transferred from it to the processing script, so let's take a look at the important `<form>` element attributes you should consider:

- `action` – The `action` attribute sets the destination to which the form data is submitted. The value of this attribute can be an absolute or relative URL.

- `method` – The `method` attribute specifies how the data is sent to the URL specified in the `action` attribute. The value of the `method` attribute can be either `POST` or `GET`, with `GET` being the default option if this attribute is left empty. We will discuss these options later in this chapter as they play vital roles in processing a form's data in PHP.

- `enctype` – This attribute specifies how the form's data is encoded when it's submitted. However, this attribute only comes into effect when the `method` attribute has been set to `POST`. `enctype` has three possible values: `application/x-222-form-urlencoded`, `multipart/form-data` and `text/plain`. The first option encodes everything that's submitted into the form, so all spaces are encoded to "+" and all other special characters are converted to ASCII Hex values. The second option encodes none of the form data. This is essential if your form has any type of file upload control or processing. The last option will convert spaces in the submitted data to "+" but won't encode any special characters. These options should be assessed when coding your form as they'll play an important role in the state of the data when it arrives at the action attribute's URL.

There are two attributes that can be set on any form element and that are also important when processing data with PHP scripts:

- `name` – The `name` attribute value is an identifier used to collect the data when it's sent to the destination URL. For example, if we have the element `<input type="text" name="data" />`, the value entered for it by the user becomes available in an array on the server and can be referenced using the array key `'data'`.

- `value` – The `value` attribute is where the information or data for each element in the form is set. You can use this attribute to set a default value for an element.

Here's an example form using some of the attributes outlined above:

```
<form method="post">
    <input name="myField" value="Hello World" />
    <button type="submit">submit</button>
</form>
```

So far we've only looked at the important parts of forms that come into play when using them in PHP. However, you may find yourself using attributes and tags that haven't been listed here. The elements we've discussed cover the basics, so if you're hungry for more information on forms, feel free to hit up these external references:

- http://reference.sitepoint.com/html/elements-form

- http://www.tizag.com/htmlT/forms.php

- http://www.htmlgoodies.com/tutorials/forms/article.php/3479121/So-You-Want-A-Form-Huh.htm

POST and GET

Each form's `method` attribute allows only two options, `POST` and `GET`. As we know, PHP has some special predefined variables such as the `$_SESSION` variable. PHP also has two other predefined variables which are designed to collect data ultimately sent by HTML forms, `$_POST` and `$_GET`, but these variables can also be used in other ways—something we'll take a look at later on.

For now, let's illustrate the difference between `POST` and `GET` with an example. Create some new files in our experiments folder: **form.php** and **collect.php**. In our **form.php** file, add the following code:

```
<html>
<body>
    <form method="post" action="collect.php">
        <h1>Form #1</h1>
        <input name="data" placeholder="enter a string"
➥type="text" />
        <button type="submit">submit</button>
    </form>
    <form method="get" action="collect.php">
        <h1>Form #2</h1>
        <input name="data" placeholder="enter a string"
➥type="text" />
```

```
        <button type="submit">submit</button>
    </form>
</body>
</html>
```

Done that? Good. Now go ahead and add the following code to the **collect.php** file:

```php
<?php
if (!empty($_POST['data'])) {
    echo 'The following string was sent from form #1: ' .
➥$_POST['data'];
} elseif (!empty($_GET['data'])) {
    echo 'The following string was sent from form #2: ' .
➥$_GET['data'];
}
```

Next, open **form.php** in your browser, type something into the input field in Form #1 and hit submit. You should see something like Figure 4.2:

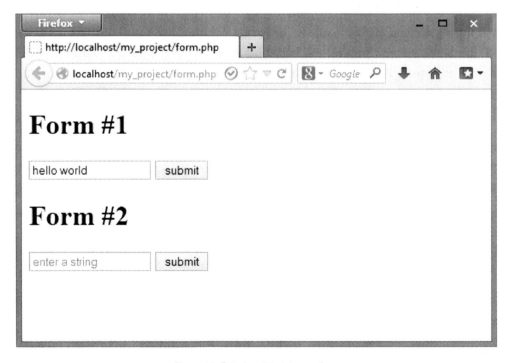

Figure 4.1. Entering data into our form

Figure 4.2. The result of submitting the form

If you fill out Form #2, as shown in Figure 4.3, and hit submit, you should see
something similar to Figure 4.4:

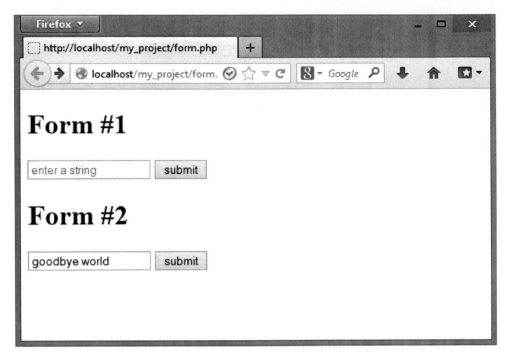

Figure 4.3. Entering data into Form #2

Figure 4.4. The result of submitting the form

The main difference between the two forms is shown if you look at the URL you're redirected to when you submit Form #2—as shown in Figure 4.5.

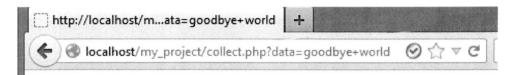

Figure 4.5. The URL the form redirects to after submission

As you can see, the string we entered into Form #2 has been placed into the URL, along with some other pieces of code. This is what we call a **URL variable** and it results from a form submitted with the GET method. The POST method, on the other hand, sends the data between the pages silently, behind the scenes. Using this method, the user sees no evidence of their data, except when the string is displayed in their browser by the **collect.php** file.

Because the data is present in the URL as a variable before being submitted to the **collect.php** script, the GET method is less secure than the POST method. As such, if you have hidden input fields in your form—such as identification data or authorization data—you would want to use the POST method rather than the GET method. In fact, in most cases when developing a web app, you will want to use the POST method for transferring data. This is because, with the GET method, any data can be injected into the URL variable.

For example, if we navigate to the **collect.php** file in our browser, we should see a blank screen. Now in the URL bar, after **collect.php** let's add `?data=hello%20world%20I%20have%20been%20injected`. If we then load this new URL, we can see that the injected data in the URL is being displayed on screen. Now, our example is not that alarming and may seem kind of cool, but actually this is a tame example of a potentially risky issue.

Imagine that we have a form that looks like Figure 4.6.

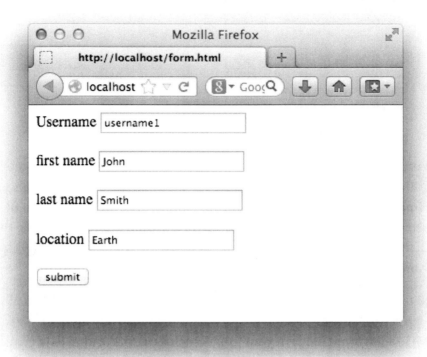

Figure 4.6. A form at risk of tampering

When this form is submitted, it sends data to a database. The form also contains a hidden input element that holds data detailing the user's ID in the database. We have used a GET method for this form so, when it's submitted, our browser would show a URL like:

```
http://www.ourdomain.com/savedata.php?userid=1&name=user&bio=
➥hello%20world
```

Can you see the risk? A malicious person could change the userid URL variable to a different user's identifier, and alter the name or bio URL variable. The result? That user's information will have been changed without them authorizing it, or even knowing it's taken place.

Form Action with PHP

We've looked at some simple examples of using forms, and the basic use of $_POST and $_GET, but there's more to processing forms with PHP than just these two variables.

To begin with, let's take a quick look at PHP_SELF. As we've discussed, PHP has special predefined variables, which we can use throughout our scripts to do some very special things. A group of these variables, however, are even more special than the rest. They're located within the $_SERVER array, which hold server and execution environment information, such as headers, paths, and script locations on the server. We can access these pieces of data just as we would with any other array. One of the keys in the $_SERVER array is PHP_SELF, which holds information on the current PHP file being accessed in relation to the document root.

To see this PHP_SELF value in action, let's create a new file in our **experiments** folder called **self.php**. In this file, add the following code:

```php
<?php
echo $_SERVER['PHP_SELF'];
```

Now, when you view this file in your browser, you should see the URL to the file **self.php** relative to your server's document root.

In our case this'd be something similar to "localhost/experiments/self.php". We can use 'PHP_SELF' in our form's action attribute to make it submit to **self.php**, and there we can use the $_POST or $_GET variables to check if the form has transferred the data, and then execute code to process it further.

An example of this would be:

```php
<?php
if (!empty($_POST['data'])) {
    echo 'Form has been submitted';
    // code to process data from form
}
?>
<html>
<body>
    <form action="POST" action="<?php echo $_SERVER
```

```
➥['PHP_SELF']; ?>">
        <input type="text" name="data" type="text"
➥placeholder="Type in a string here" />
        <button type="submit">submit</button>
    </form>
</body>
</html>
```

When the form is submitted, PHP detects this and executes the echo command, which displays the "Form has been submitted" string in our browser. The PHP_SELF variable is very useful for forms that need to submit to the same script that displays them and, upon submission, execute code to handle the data.

When using the PHP_SELF variable as your form's action, it's important to use the htmlspecialchars() function to filter any unwanted characters from the URL to help prevent Cross Site Scripting (XSS) attacks. To implement this in our example above, you'd change the form tag to look like the following:

```
<form action="POST" action="<?php echo htmlspecialchars
➥($_SERVER['PHP_SELF']); ?>">
```

For more information on improving the security of your PHP scripts and protecting against XSS vulnerabilities, please check out the following articles:

▨ http://seancoates.com/blogs/xss-woes

▨ http://blog.astrumfutura.com/tag/xss/

Superglobals and $_REQUEST

$_POST and $_GET belong to specific group of variables known as **superglobal variables**. Superglobals are specially-defined variables—normally arrays—that are built into PHP and can be accessed in any script at any point. They're called superglobals because they can be accessed anywhere, and at any time. The $_SERVER variable we discussed in the previous section is also part of the superglobal family of variables, along with some others that we haven't discussed yet.

Another member of the superglobal family is the $_REQUEST variable. It's a little different from other superglobals, such as $_POST and $_GET. Indeed, $_REQUEST is unusual because its keys are created by all values generated in the current HTTP request by the user's browser. This means that all data stored in the $_GET variable and the $_POST variable can be accessed by $_REQUEST.

In addition, any data stored using browser cookies is also stored in $_REQUEST. At first, you may think this could be very useful, but it actually poses a very significant security risk, specifically because it can access data from cookies in PHP. Having a superglobal that can be accessed anywhere in PHP, and which can also gather cookie data is like have a ticking time bomb sitting in your PHP code.

I strongly advise not using $_REQUEST, and to ensure none of your PHP code is accessing it. This will remove the risk of malicious attacks manipulating the script accessing the superglobal to access your users' sensitive cookie data.

php.ini is set up by default to not include cookie data in $_REQUEST, but if your host has edited PHP's php.ini configuration file, they may have changed the default setting. It's strongly advised not to access cookie data through the $_REQUEST superglobal; the safest method is to turn off access to cookie data in php.ini. For more information on the $_REQUEST superglobal, including examples of it in use, and an overview of the risks entailed in using it, please see the PHP manual's resource page.[1]

Forms and Databases

Given what we've discussed previously, it may seem to you like GET is the bad guy, but it can actually be quite useful in a variety of ways. As we've discussed, GET will pass form field values as parameters in the URL, which, in turn, can be used by a PHP script to create dynamic data.

So far, we've looked at data taken from a URL, which has been created by a form. However we can also use GET without a form to generate a dynamic URL. This can be useful in many situations. For example, if we want to load a blog post in the front-end of our application, we can collect a post's id from a specifically written URL using the $_GET variable, and then pass on that id to our script to collect the specific post from the database.

To try this out, we first need to open phpMyAdmin and create a new database called testposts, ensuring we have selected a user from our list who's already set up in phpMyAdmin to have full privileges to it.

---

[1] http://php.net/manual/en/reserved.variables.request.php

Next we create a new table called `posts`, which can be done either through the PDO MySQL script, or by using phpMyAdmin.

Our table `posts` will only need two columns for the purposes of this example: `id` and `content`. The `id` column should be set as the `PRIMARY` index key with `AUTO_INCREMENT` enabled, and its type set to `INT`, while the `content` column is set as `LONGTEXT`.

Once the table has been created, we need to place a test post into it. Add an entry, placing some dummy copy into the `content` column. Feel free to add some paragraph HTML tags where appropriate. A unique id should be generated for this entry automatically.

 Use Basic HTML Formatting for the Content in Your Database

You should only use basic HTML formatting tags in your database. Complex HTML or any other browser processed coding language can cause security issues.

Now let's create a new file in our web experiment folder called **post.php**. Let's imagine that we have the following URL: `localhost/experiments/post.php?id=1` where the `id` URL variable represents the post id. In this case, the post has an id of 1, and `experiments` is the name of the folder where we'll be creating this example.

In our **post.php** file, add the following code:

```php
<?php
class Posts {
    public $db = '';
    public function __construct() {
        $this->db = new PDO("mysql:host=localhost;dbname=kickstart",
➥"root", "i8vfbxdb");
        $this->db->setAttribute(PDO::ATTR_ERRMODE,
➥ PDO::ERRMODE_EXCEPTION);
        $this->index();
    }
    public function index() {
        $id = 0;
        $posts = array();
        $template = '';
        if (!empty($_GET['id'])) {
            $id = $_GET['id'];
```

```
        }
        try {
            if (!empty($id)) {
                $query = $this->db->prepare("SELECT * FROM posts
➡WHERE id = ?");
                $params = array($id);
                $template = 'single-post.php';
            } else {
                $query = $this->db->prepare("SELECT * FROM posts");
                $params = array();
                $template = 'list-posts.php';
            }
            $query->execute($params);
            for ($i = 0; $row = $query->fetch(); $i++) {
                $posts[] = array('id' => $row['id'], 'content' =>
➡ $row['content']);
            }
        } catch (PDOException $e) {
            echo $e->getMessage();
        }
        $query->closeCursor();
        $db = null;
        require_once($template);
    }
}
$posts = new Posts();
?>
```

What we've done here is is to create a new class, Posts. At the start we initiated our PDO MySQL connection. We then move onto the index method, in which we check to see if the URL has a URL variable and, if so, we collect it from the URL, as well as attempt to collect the post with the same id from our database. If there's no URL variable, we then just load up all the posts in our database. Finally we then load the template which relates to the database query we have executed.

Next, we'll need to put together our template files to display the data we've retrieved from the database. So create two new files—one called **list-posts.php**, and the other **single-post.php**. In **list-posts.php** add the following code:

```
<h1>List of Blog Posts</h1>
<?php foreach ($posts as $post): ?>
    <h3>Post #<?php echo htmlspecialchars($post['id']); ?></h3>
```

```
    <?php echo htmlspecialchars($post['content']); ?>
    <a href="http://localhost/experiments/posts.php?id=<?php echo
➥htmlspecialchars($post['id']); ?>">Read More</a>
    <hr/>
<?php endforeach; ?>
```

Finally in our **single-post.php** file add this code:

```
<?php foreach($posts as $post): ?>
    <h1>Post #<?php echo htmlspecialchars($post['id']); ?></h1>
    <hr/>
    <?php echo htmlspecialchars($post['content']); ?>
    <a href="http://localhost/experiments/posts.php">
➥Back to Post List</a>
<?php endforeach; ?>
```

Now, if we navigate to our **posts.php** file we can see there's a list of posts—or a single post in this case, as we currently only have one in the database—each of which has a link for us to "Read More". Clicking on this link takes us to the individual post page, and displays a different template than the one used to view the full list of posts.

This is a very short example, showing how the $_GET variable allows us to dynamically load blog posts, and interact with our database. We could easily change the example to use the $_POST variable instead. However, we wouldn't then be able to share URLs referring to individual posts. Instead, the URL would only send visitors to the list of posts where they must click on the "**Read More**" link themselves.

This example leads us very nicely to the next section of this chapter where we'll expand on this code snippet, along with the earlier ones, and begin to build the real guts of our blog platform.

Building on our Platform

In this section, we're going to build on the example we've just created—which displays a list of blog posts with links to read individual posts—and get that working in our application.

Let's take the existing code from above and tweak it slightly. Modify the **posts.php** file in the **includes** directory our blog platform folder so the constructor looks like this:

```php
public function __construct() {
    parent::__construct();
    $this->comments = new Comments();
    if (!empty($_GET['id'])) {
        $this->viewPost($_GET['id']);
    } else {
        $this->getPosts();
    }
}
```

With this code, our constructor checks to see if there's a URL variable called id. If there is, it proceeds to collect the data from the variable, and pass it to the view-Post() method within the Blog class. If there isn't a URL variable called id, the application is, instead, told to load up all the posts from our database. This'll allow visitors to see all of our posts, and then click on a link to view an individual post.

The next change that we'll make to the posts.php file is to edit is the getPosts() method:

```php
public function getPosts() {
    $id = 0;
    $posts = $return = array();
    $template = '';
    $query = $this->ksdb->db->prepare("SELECT * FROM posts");
    try {
        $query->execute();
        for ($i = 0; $row = $query->fetch(); $i++) {
            $return[$i] = array();
            foreach ($row as $key => $rowitem) {
                $return[$i][$key] = $rowitem;
            }
        }
    } catch (PDOException $e) {
        echo $e->getMessage();
    }
    $posts = $return;
```

```
    $template = 'list-posts.php';
    include_once 'frontend/templates/' . $template;
}
```

The getPosts() method is used to collect all the posts from the database to create a list of them for visitors to our blog. It uses the PDO database functionality from the database.php file in the **includes** folder. This allows us to write our own database query through PDO. Using this method we want to load all the rows from the posts table with the SELECT * FROM posts database query. We then use the try and catch exception handling routine in an attempt to run the query. If it's successful, we then loop through the array returned from the database and add the result to a new key in the $return array. If it fails, we echo the error message from PDO that tells us what's wrong with our database query. Finally, we load the list-posts.php template.

 Displaying PDO Error Messages

Echoing PDO error messages, as we've done in the example above, can be helpful during development, as it'll help us track down with issues our databse queries. However, you should definitely not echo PDO error messages in production applications—doing so can be a security risk.

The last step for this class is to edit the viewPost() method:

```
public function viewPost($postId) {
    $id = $postId;
    $posts = $return = array();
    $template = '';
    $query = $this->ksdb->db->prepare
➥("SELECT * FROM posts WHERE id = ?");
    try {
        $query->execute(array($id));
        for ($i = 0; $row = $query->fetch(); $i++) {
            $return[$i] = array();
            foreach ($row as $key => $rowitem) {
                $return[$i][$key] = $rowitem;
            }
        }
    } catch (PDOException $e) {
        echo $e->getMessage();
    }
```

```
    $posts = $return;
    $posts[0]['content'] = $posts[0]['content'];
    $template = 'view-post.php';
    include_once 'frontend/templates/'.$template;
}
```

In a nutshell, the `viewPost()` method displays individual blog posts to our blog's visitors.Our application uses it to load the data for a particular post, based on data from a URL variable. It requires that `$postId` is passed to the method once it's called, which we've done with the class's constructor. This method uses the PDO database functionality to load a specific post from the database based on the `id` of the posts stored in the database. In addition, our script uses a `try` ... `catch` exception handler to check if the database query is successful. If the query is successful, we'll again loop through the array returned from the database, and assign the data returned to a key in the `$return` array. If it fails, we show the database error generated by PDO, as before. Finally, we load up the `view-post.php` template..

In the methods described above, we're loading some template files— so we need to go ahead and create them. Now, we could build the template files from scratch, but for the purposes of this project, we'll design and build them using the Twitter Bootstrap Framework[2]. Bootstrap is fantastic for getting web applications' UI elements up and running incredibly quickly, freeing you to focus on the task of building the back-end of an amazing application.

If you're comfortable with setting up Bootstrap yourself, go ahead and implement it into the project as you see fit. If you're unsure about the process, don't worry—copy everything from the **includes** folder in this book's code archive, and you'll be up and running with Twitter Bootstrap in no time.

Go back to our project and create two new files in the **templates** folder in the **frontend** folder and title them **list-posts.php** and **view-post.php**. In **list-posts.php** add the following code:

```php
<?php require_once 'includes/temps/header.php'; ?>
<?php foreach ($posts as $post): ?>
    <h3>Post #<?php echo htmlspecialchars($post['id']); ?></h3>
        <p><?php echo implode(' ', array_slice(explode(' ',
```

---

[2] http://twitter.github.io/bootstrap/index.html

```
➥strip_tags($post['content'])), 0, 10)); ?> [...]</p>
        <a href="<?php echo $this->base->url."/?id=".$post['id'];
➥ ?>" class="btn btn-primary">Read More</a>
    <hr/>
<?php endforeach; ?>
<?php require_once 'includes/temps/footer.php'; ?>
```

Next, add the following code to the **view-post.php** file:

```
<?php require_once 'includes/temps/header.php'; ?>
<br/>
<a href="<?php echo $this->base->url; ?>" class="btn btn-primary">
➥Return to Post List</a>
<?php foreach ($posts as $post): ?>
    <h3>Post #<?php echo htmlspecialchars($post['id']); ?></h3>
        <?php echo htmlspecialchars($post['content']); ?>
    <hr/>
<?php endforeach; ?>
<?php require_once 'includes/temps/footer.php'; ?>
```

Our `list-post.php` file loops through the numerous posts we have collected from our database, creating a small excerpt from our post's content and creating a link to read each one. Our `view-post.php` file displays the title and the body of content for an individual post that's been loaded from the database.

Both `list-post.php` and `view-post.php` should seem pretty straightforward. However, you may have noticed some unusual and complex-looking code in the **list-posts.php** file:

```
implode(' ', array_slice(explode(' ',
view-post.phpstrip_tags($post['content'])), 0, 10));
```

This line of code combines several different PHP functions to strip out the first ten words of our post's content to automatically create an excerpt string that'll be displayed in our list of posts. The `strip_tags()` function removes any HTML tags from the content, and the `explode()` function creates a new array and key each time the function encounters a space in the content. Next, the `array_slice()` function is used to take the first ten keys in our array created by the `explode()` function. The `array_slice()` function is passed 0 to indicate it should start counting from 0 and stop counting when it reaches 10. In addition, it's passed the array created by the explode() function. Finally we use the implode() function to bring those ten array values together as a string.

For more details about these functions in PHP and an in-depth overview of what they can be used for, check out the following resources:

- http://php.net/manual/en/function.strip-tags.php

- http://php.net/manual/en/function.explode.php

- http://php.net/manual/en/function.array-slice.php

- http://php.net/manual/en/function.implode.php

The next stage in our example application is to create our admin and login panels. We'll create the latter first. Open up the **login.php** file in the **includes** directory. It's located within our project directory's main directory. Start by adding the following to the constructor method:

```
public function __construct() {
    $this->ksdb = new Database;
    $this->base = (object) '';
    $this->base->url = "http://".$_SERVER['SERVER_NAME'];
    $this->index();
}
```

In essence, our constructor sets up the objects and variables we're going to need throughout the class. Next we need to add to the index() method:

```
public function index() {
    if ($_SERVER['REQUEST_METHOD'] === 'POST') {
        $this->validateDetails();
    } elseif (!empty($_GET['status']) && $_GET['status'] ==
➥'inactive') {
        $error = 'You have been logged out due to inactivity.
➥ Please log in again.';
    }
    require_once 'admin/templates/loginform.php';
}
```

In the index() method, we check to see whether our user has been logged out due to inactivity. It does this by checking to see if the inactive URL variable has been set. It also checks to see if form data has been passed to it using the POST method and, if so, the script then assumes that a user is trying to log in and will fire up the validateDetails() method to check their login details—something we'll cover shortly. Finally, the method loads up loginform.php, which is used to load the form for users to log in with.

Next we move onto the loginSuccess() method and the loginFail() method:

```php
public function loginSuccess() {
    header('Location: http://' . $_SERVER['SERVER_NAME'] .
➥ '/admin/posts.php');
    return;
}

public function loginFail() {
    return 'Your Username/Password was incorrect';
}
```

The loginSuccess() method is used in those instances when the login is successful, and the method redirects the user to the admin panel, and the loginFail() method returns an error status (informing the user that their login was unsuccessful.)

For more information on the header() function, please see http://php.net/manual/en/function.header.php.

Finally, we'll move on to the validateDetails() method:

```php
private function validateDetails() {
    if (!empty($_POST['username']) && !empty($_POST['password'])) {
        $salt = '$2a$07$R.gJb2U2N.FmZ4hPp1y2CN$';
        $password = crypt($_POST['password'], $salt);
        $return = array();
        $query = $this->ksdb->db->prepare("SELECT * FROM users WHERE
➥username = ? AND password = ?");
        try {
            $query->execute(array($_POST['username'], $password));
            for ($i = 0; $row = $query->fetch(); $i++) {
                $return[$i] = array();
                foreach ($row as $key => $rowitem) {
                    $return[$i][$key] = $rowitem;
                }
            }
```

```
        } catch (PDOException $e) {
            echo $e->getMessage();
        }
        if (!empty($return) && !empty($return[0])) {
            $this->loginSuccess();
        } else {
            echo $error = $this->loginFail();
        }
    }
}
```

validateDetails() is the core method within the login class, and is where our script checks and validates the user's attempt to log in to our blog application's admin panel.

To start with, the method checks that the script has obtained form data using the POST method, and checks that the username and password keys are present in the $_POST superglobal variable and are not empty, using the empty() function in PHP. If the username and password are in the $_POST superglobal variable, we then create a password **salt**[3] made up of random characters and symbols used to encrypt our password. We then take the submitted passwords from the login form, encrypt it, and then check to see if the submitted username and encrypted password match the details stored in the database.

Now that we have our login class created, we just need to create a template for our login form. Create a directory named **templates** in the **admin** folder, and add a new PHP file called **loginform.php**.

 A Note on Structure

It's worth taking the time to create a new header and footer template file for the admin section. Separating the front-end header and footer template files will save complication when differentiating between the front-end and the admin panel. Please see the project's file structure for more details about setting this up.

In the **loginform.php** file, add the following code:

---

[3] http://en.wikipedia.org/wiki/Salt_(cryptography)

```php
<?php require_once 'includes/temps/header.php'; ?>
<br/>
<?php if (!empty($error)): ?>
    <div class="alert alert-error">~<?php echo $error; ?></div>
<?php endif; ?>
<br/>
<form action="<?php echo htmlspecialchars($_SERVER['PHP_SELF']); ?>"
➥ method="post" class="form-horizontal offset2">
    <h3>Admin Login</h3>
    <div class="control-group <?php echo (!empty($error)?
➥ 'error': ''); ?>">
        <label class="control-label" for="inputEmail">Username
➥</label>
        <div class="controls">
            <input type="text" name="username" id="inputEmail"
➥placeholder="Username">
        </div>
    </div>
    <div class="control-group <?php echo (!empty($error)? 'error':
➥ ''); ?>">
        <label class="control-label" for="inputPassword">Password
➥</label>
        <div class="controls">
            <input type="password" name="password"
➥id="inputPassword" placeholder="Password">
        </div>
    </div>
    <div class="control-group">
        <div class="controls">
            <button type="submit" class="btn">Sign in</button>
        </div>
    </div>
</form>
<?php require_once 'includes/temps/footer.php'; ?>
```

In this file, we've created a form, which prompts the user for a username and a password to log in to the admin section of our application. When this form is submitted, it will send its data to the same file our login class will use to handle the login process. It'll then send back any errors, along with the user, to this login file.

Now that we have our login panel and login class created, we just need to create the admin panel and its required classes. In the **includes** directory again, open the file admin.php file and add the following:

```
class Adminpanel {
    public function __construct() {
        $this->ksdb = new Database;
        $this->base = (object) '';
        $this->base->url = "http://".$_SERVER['SERVER_NAME'];
    }
}
```

Here we've added code to the constructor in the Adminpanel class, which contains objects and variables we're going to use throughout the admin.php file. This is the main class that the other classes in the admin file are going to extend.

Next, we are going to add code to the listPosts() method:

```
public function listPosts() {
    $posts = $return = array();
    $query = $this->ksdb->db->prepare("SELECT * FROM posts");
    try {
        $query->execute();
        for ($i = 0; $row = $query->fetch(); $i++) {
            $return[$i] = array();
            foreach ($row as $key => $rowitem) {
                $return[$i][$key] = $rowitem;
            }
        }
    } catch (PDOException $e) {
        echo $e->getMessage();
    }
    $posts = $return;
    require_once 'templates/manageposts.php';
}
```

The listPosts() method is almost exactly the same as the getPosts() method from the posts.php file: We load all the posts from the posts table in the database and check the query. If the check is OK, we get the data from the database and add it to the $return array. If not, we show the database error. Finally, we load the manageposts.php template file.

Now, we move onto the addPost() method:

```php
public function addPost() {
    require_once 'templates/newpost.php';
}
```

This simply loads the newpost.php template.

Finally, we add to the savePost() method:

```php
public function savePost() {
    $array = $format = $return = array();
    if (!empty($_POST['post'])) {
        $post = $_POST['post'];
    }
    if (!empty($post['content'])) {
        $array['content'] = $post['content'];
        $format[] = ':content';
    }
    $cols = $values = '';
    $i = 0;
    foreach ($array as $col => $data) {
        if ($i == 0) {
            $cols .= $col;
            $values .= $format[$i];
        } else {
            $cols .= ',' . $col;
            $values .= ',' . $format[$i];
        }
        $i++;
    }
    try {
        $query = $this->ksdb->db->prepare("INSERT INTO posts
(".$cols.") VALUES (".$values.")");
        for($c=0;$c<$i;$c++){
            $query->bindParam($format[$c], ${'var'.$c});
        }
        $z=0;
        foreach($array as $col => $data){
            ${'var' . $z} = $data;
            $z++;
        }
        $result = $query->execute();
        $add = $query->rowCount();
    } catch (PDOException $e) {
        echo $e->getMessage();
```

```
    }
    $query->closeCursor();
    $this->db = null;
    if (!empty($add)) {
        $status = array('success' => 'Your post has been saved
➥successfully.');
    } else {
        $status = array('error' => 'There has been an error saving
➥your post. Please try again later.');
    }
    header("Location: http://localhost/kickstart/admin/posts.php");
}
```

The savePost() method uses the PDO database functionality to prepare an INSERT SQL query to save data to the posts table in our database. We then return a status depending on whether the data has saved to the database correctly or not. Here we're using the insert methods we spoke about in Chapter 2.

All we have to do now is to create a couple more templates. We'll add two new PHP files to the **templates** folder inside the **admin** directory. The first file, **manageposts.php**, is where we see a list of all the posts saved in our database, while the other, **newpost.php**, is where we have a very simple form in which we can enter data to create content for a new blog post. In the **manageposts.php** file, add the following code:

```
<?php require_once '_inc/header.php'; ?>
<a href="<?php echo $this->base->url; ?>/posts.php?action=create"
➥class="btn btn-info">Create Post</a>
<table>
    <thead>
        <tr>
            <td>Post Title</td>
            <td>Post Content</td>
            <td>Actions</td>
        </tr>
    </thead>
    <tbody>
    <?php foreach($posts as $post): ?>
        <tr>
            <td><h3>Post #<?php echo htmlspecialchars($post['id']);
➥ ?></h3></td>
            <td><p><?php echo implode(' ', array_slice(explode(' ',
```

```
➥ strip_tags($post['content'])), 0, 10)); ?> [...]</p></td>
            <td><a href="<?php echo $this->base->url."/posts.php
➥?id=".$post['id']."&action=edit"; ?>" class="btn btn-primary">
➥Edit Post</a><a href="<?php echo $this->base->url."/?id=".
➥$post['id']."&action=delete"; ?>" class="btn btn-primary">
➥Delete Post</a></td>
        </tr>
    <?php endforeach; ?>
    </tbody>
</table>
<?php require_once '_inc/footer.php'; ?>
```

Here we can see the use of the strip_tags(), explode(), array_slice() and implode() methods combined together to create a short excerpt for our post, as well as the foreach loop to iterate over all the posts that are collected from our database.

Next, open up the **newpost.php** file and add the following code:

```
<?php require_once '_inc/header.php'; ?>
    <form action="<?php echo $this->base->url.'
➥/posts.php?action=save'; ?>"method="POST">
    <h3>
    New Post
    </h3>
            <div class="control-group">

    <label class="control-label" for="content">Content</label>
    <div class="controls">
                    <textarea name="post[content]" id="content">
➥</textarea>
                </div>
            </div>
            <div class="control-group">
                <div class="controls">
                    <button type="submit" class="btn">
    Save Post
    </button>
                </div>
            </div>
        </form>
 <?php require_once '_inc/footer.php'; ?>
```

At this point, we only have a basic text area for typing content. Later on, we'll be expanding this panel further to include an area for a post title, and change the text area into a more dynamic and usable content editor.

After all the code above has been added to the **newpost.php** file, you should now have a working admin panel where you can create new blog posts!

We're also able to access the public, or front-end, section of our project, view a list of blog posts, and click on an individual post to read its content, as shown in Figure 4.7. Exciting, huh?

Figure 4.7. The front-end of our project

Feel free to navigate to the project's main **index.php** file and start using the system.

In the next chapter we will extend the admin panel further to allow us to update existing blog posts in the database and also to delete blog posts.

Summary

Forms are a vital part of any web application, enabling users to submit data. PHP provides us with powerful tools for processing, storing and working with the data submitted via forms. In this chapter, we've discussed the ways PHP can collect the data submitted from a form, looked at the POST and GET methods, and also discussed how to validate the data collected, preparing it for entry into our MySQL database. We then used the form methods we had discussed to build out our blog application.

Chapter 5

Sessions and Cookies

As we've discussed, databases are ideal for storing permanently storing data that an application can retrieve at a later date. There are, however, some options for storing data on a more temporary basis with PHP. **Cookies** and **sessions** are designed to hold smaller chunks of data than would normally be held in a database. They're often used to hold users' personal data for login functionality, for example, and to provide quick access to user data for functionality like application profiles.

The big difference between cookies and sessions is where the data is stored. Cookies store data on the client's computer, while sessions store their data on the web server. PHP can work with both cookies and sessions, and we'll take a closer look at each of these options in detail in this chapter.

Cookies: Overview

HTTP requests are stateless, which means that every time a new page is requested by a browser, data relevant to a previous request from the user isn't remembered by the web server.

Fortunately we have the option to use cookies, which allow us to store small pieces of information on a visitor's browser. This cookie information can be loaded by a website, and used in its scripts to personalize data, or to help create dynamic data on pages within the site.

Cookies are also incredibly useful when you need to keep data between HTTP page requests. Each cookie created in the browser is accessible only by the browser that created it, helping to keep the information contained in it secure.

 Cookies and Recent European Legislation

Recently, cookies have been placed under a blanket of doubt for web developers who live, or work with projects that are to be deployed, in Europe. The European Union has the opinion that cookies are being used to store too much personal information about visitors to websites, and new legislation[1] has been put in place with the aim of making their use more transparent.

This legislation doesn't mean developers shouldn't use cookies, but it does mean we're having to use them more efficiently, and only use them when their application has a real need.

The truth is, most cookies used by websites are harmless—with many used simply to enhance content for users based on personal information they've readily given to the site.

Sessions: Overview

Useful as they are, cookies do have a vulnerability—because they're stored on a user's computer, they can, in theory, be tampered with by the user or, even worse, by a virus on the user's computer. Sessions offer an alternative to cookies and come without the client-side security risk.

Sessions are a special form of continuity used to store data across page requests as a user navigates during their visit to your website. When you log into a web application, edit some content, and log out, more often than not, a session will have been working away behind the scenes.

---

[1] http://www.ico.org.uk/for_organisations/privacy_and_electronic_communications/the_guide/cookies

It's worth noting that sessions still rely on cookies to successfully attribute data stored in a session on the website's server to the client. To put it another way, a cookie on the client's computer is required to identify them each time they visit the website.

Session Vs Cookies

As you're developing in PHP you can use both cookies and sessions without much difficulty. Both can be accessed using very simple methods in any script. Before we dive into any code, though, it's important to explore cookies' and sessions' unique features to better understand when you might favor one over the other.

Cookies

The first unique feature of cookies—as opposed to sessions—is that we give them an expiry date. When clients leave our website or web application and wander off to other parts of the Internet, there's a good chance that they may return at some point. With cookies we can set an expiry date so that, when the user does visit again, as long as the expiry date hasn't passed, information they submitted or entered before can be displayed as if they've never been away.

A good example of the use of expiry dates is when you log into a social media application, like Facebook. After logging in, you might navigate to another site. But return to Facebook within a certain time period and you may discover that you're still logged in. The cookie provides Facebook with a piece of data that helps it to load up our profile, which improves the user experience hugely. Giving cookies an expiry date makes this convenience to the user possible while adding a layer of security. By obliging users to re-authenticate after a certain period of inactivity has passed, other users are prevented from accessing the data stored in the cookie through means of hardware hijacking.

Another feature unique to cookies is that, each time someone visits a website that has created a cookie on their machine, the cookie is automatically included in subsequent HTTP requests sent by the client. With this in mind, it's important not to have your cookies store too much data as they'll be using the web server's bandwidth.

Cookies make data management simpler as using them doesn't require any form of database for storing the data or the cookie. This, in turn, means you don't need any skill or knowledge in database management to use cookies. Furthermore, in many web programming languages, such as PHP, functionality for creating, assigning data, and accessing cookies is already built in, so you don't have to worry about building your own library to access them.

Overall, cookies should be used to store small pieces of information that can be used to personalize small parts of a web page to improve a user's experience. They can also be used to allow users to resume their previous interaction with your application, creating the illusion that they're still logged in.

 Cookies and Security

It's important to remember not to store sensitive data in cookies due to the fact they're sent to the web server each time a page request is made, and can be accessed by tech-savvy computer attackers.

In addition, because they're stored on the user's computer, there's very little we, as developers, can do to protect the cookies. Because of this, cookies should ideally only store data that can be used by an application to identify information that's stored in databases or other secure storage options, as opposed to storing the data in the cookie itself.

Sessions

Sessions combine the usefulness of cookies with the security and manageability of the web server. Unlike with a cookie, specific variable data and information is not directly stored on the user's computer. The data itself is actually stored on the web server that houses and processes the website or web application.

Sessions are very unlike any other variables we have looked at so far, as they don't pass the data directly between the pages requested by the browser—instead, the data is retrieved from the session we initiate at the beginning of each page. As mentioned previously, sessions use a cookie stored on the client's computer to identity the correct user with their data stored in a session. This cookie doesn't hold any personal information, nor does the data make any sense unless compared with the data stored on the web server; usually it comes in the form of a key such as `350401be75bbb0fafd3d912a1a1d5e54`. For this reason, the data security of sessions is of a higher level than when using cookies alone.

While this method of storing data on both the client's computer and the server may seem a bit clumsy, it actually has its advantages:

- Sessions don't have a limit on the amount of data you can store in them. This is because sessions are stored on the server so they don't impact negatively on the server's bandwidth.

- Because session data is stored on a web server and not on the user's computer, this allows you to focus your security efforts on your web server, rather than applying encryption methods which fit into the storage capabilities of user's browser.

One thing to remember with sessions is that you can specify how long they stay alive, or active. We call this "time-to-live" and it's usually configured for the session to expire or die after a user has closed the browser or tab that initiated the session with the web server. So, for example, if a user logs into a social media application, when they are finished using it and close their browser, the session, if configured to do so, will automatically remove its data for that user—a very useful feature.

Sessions and Cookies in PHP

Now that we've covered the reasons for using sessions and cookies, as well as the main differences between them, it's time we start to look at how to implement them in PHP.

Both sessions and cookies can be accessed and loaded by special variables dedicated to these particular methods. In PHP, we express the intent to use and manipulate a cookie by using the superglobal variable $_COOKIE. Sessions are used in a similar way through the $_SESSION superglobal.

First, let's focus on writing and using cookies.

Cookies in PHP

There are special functions we must use to assign data to cookies. Let's create a new file in our **experiments** folder and name it **storage.php**. Once this file has been created, add the following code to it:

```php
<?php
$expire = time() + 60 * 60 * 24 * 30;
➡// This equals to the time now plus 30 days in the future
setcookie("user", "Joe Public", $expire);
if (isset($_COOKIE["user"])) {
    echo "Welcome " . $_COOKIE["user"] . "!";
} else {
    echo "Welcome guest!";
}
```

isset()

The **isset()** function checks to see if a variable or element has been assigned a value. In the code above, **isset()** will make sure a key in **$_COOKIE** has a value before letting the **if** statement continue.

If you now take your browser and navigate to the **storage.php** file, you can see that our script hasn't detected our "Joe Public" name, and actually thinks we're a guest. This is because the cookie is set by the **setcookie()** function—this tells PHP to set a cookie in our browser along with the data to be stored, and the cookie's lifespan, after the PHP engine has rendered the whole PHP script first. When we first access the script with our code in the browser, there'll be no cookie for PHP to detect and retrieve data from. That's because the PHP will be processed on our server. However, the cookie is being set in our browser—that happens after the server is finished processing our PHP script. Therefore, we won't see the cookie's data the first time we load the page.

Refresh the **storage.php** file, and we'll see that the cookie's data has now been collected by PHP, and is displaying the "Joe Public" data we entered into the **setcookie()** function. You may also notice that the first argument passed into this function is the name argument, which sets the name of the cookie. We then use this argument to tell PHP which individual cookie we want to load in order to obtain the data we want from it. The second argument, as we've already covered, is the data we want to store in this cookie. In our example above, it's the string "Joe Public". The last argument in the function is where we set how long we want the cookie to stay alive. Usually cookies are required to have a lifespan set—a time and date after which the browser will destroy them. However, it's worth remembering that cookies used by sessions don't require a specific time-to-live date or time as theirs is controlled by the session's time-to-live.

In our code, we set the expiration time and date for the cookie, and stored it in the $expire variable, located in the first line of our code. Note we have used the time() PHP function. This allows us to obtain the time and date when our script is visited by a browser and rendered by PHP. The time() function actually returns the number of seconds that have elapsed since midnight GMT Jan 1 1970 as a number. So, instead of returning a date in a readable format, such as "May 14 12:50", time() returns a number, such as 1368553800. For more information on the time() and date() functions in PHP, please see the PHP manual's documentation[2].

It's also important to note that data from cookies will be sent to the server on every page request. If your script sends out HTML before your script sends out any cookie data, or sets any cookie data to be sent to the server, PHP will throw an error. It's important to make sure that you set and send your cookie data at the start of your script. However, you can retrieve data from a cookie further on in your script, after HTML has been sent to the browser. This will not throw a PHP error (as long as the cookie exists and has data). I highly suggest you take the time to read my SitePoint article for further reading on cookies in PHP[3].

Sessions in PHP

Now that we know the basics of how to write and use cookies, we're going to look at how to use and write sessions. Just like cookies, this method makes use of a special superglobal variable, with which we assign data to, and obtain data from, sessions: $_SESSION.

Sessions work in a similar way to cookies, but have a specific process for assigning data that's quite different from the way a cookie's data is set. Initially, we need to tell PHP we'd like to use a session, which we do with the session_start() function. We also have the option to remove session variables individually, and collectively, using functions such as session_unset() and session_destroy(). Here is a basic example of how we start a session, add data to it, and retrieve that data using the $_SESSION variable we spoke about earlier:

---

[2] http://php.net/manual/en/book.datetime.php
[3] http://www.sitepoint.com/php-sessions/

```php
<?php
session_start();
$_SESSION["username"] = "myusername";
echo "Username = " . htmlspecialchars($_SESSION["username"]);
```

As you can see, we start the session, create a new session variable titled `username` and set the string `"myusername"` to that variable. Finally, we display the string stored in the session variable in the browser. This is only a basic example because, if we were using this code in a real project,we'd actually spread it over two files—the first starting the session and creating the `username` session variable, and a second also starting a session, but then displaying the string stored in the session variable.

It's important that you end a session when you've finished using it. Despite the fact that sessions are used for temporary data storage, they can still be vulnerable to attack. Ending a session helps to ensure maximum security when dealing with potentially sensitive information. To do this, we simply add the `session_destroy()` function to our code once we are finished, like so:

```php
<?php
session_start();
$_SESSION["username"] = "Username";
echo "Username = " . $_SESSION["username"];
session_destroy();
```

It's highly recommended that you end a session once you're finished and have no further need for it in your code, in order to stop malicious code being injected into your PHP scripts.

If we don't want to end the session but, instead, remove a piece of data from it, we can use the `unset()` function. Here's an example of `unset()` in action:

```php
<?php
session_start();
unset($_SESSION["username"]);
```

We can also unset all sessions and their values by using the `session_unset()` function. So, if we change our short example from the above, we can use `session_unset()` like so:

```php
<?php
session_start();
session_unset();
```

 Don't Keep Sensitive Data in Sessions

Earlier in the chapter we discussed how cookies shouldn't be used to store sensitive data, even temporarily. That same advice can also be applied to sessions, even though they're considered more secure than cookies. While sessions' data is stored on the web server and not on the user's computer, sessions can also be a target for attackers and hackers. As such it's also recommended that you don't use sessions to store sensitive data.

Project

So now that we've covered the use of sessions and cookies, it's time we started filling out the shell of our project so it becomes a fully functional blog platform. To begin with, let's start by taking our **login.php** file in the `includes` folder, and adding to it. We'll start by editing the `index()` method:

```php
public function index() {
    if (!empty($_GET['status']) && $_GET['status'] == 'logout') {
        session_unset();
        session_destroy();
        $error = 'You have been logged out. Please log in again.';
        require_once 'admin/templates/loginform.php';
    } elseif (!empty($_SESSION['kickstart_login']) &&
➥$_SESSION['kickstart_login']) {
        header('Location: ' . $this->base->url .
➥ '/admin/posts.php');
        exit();
    } else {
        if ($_SERVER['REQUEST_METHOD'] === 'POST') {
            $this->validateDetails();
        } elseif (!empty($_GET['status'])) {
            if ($_GET['status'] == 'inactive') {
                session_unset();
                session_destroy();
                $error = 'You have been logged out due to
➥inactivity. Please log in again.';
            }
```

```
        }
        require_once 'admin/templates/loginform.php';
    }
}
```

What we've changed in the `index()` method is to introduce sessions into our login script. This use of sessions allows us to track how active our user has been in the admin panel and, if they've become idle, our application will proceed to log them out, in an attempt to increase security.

We have also added a logout process which will destroy any active session if the user has chosen to log out—again in an attempt to increase security, as well as to allow our user to take control of their session access to the admin panel.

Finally, we've also added a conditional `if` statement to check whether the user is returning to the admin panel, and if they still have an active login session. If so, our application will not ask them to log in again, improving the user experience when using our application.

Next we take a quick look at the `loginSuccess()` method:

```
public function loginSuccess() {
    $_SESSION['kickstart_login'] = true;
    $_SESSION["timeout"] = time();
    header('Location: ' . $this->base->url . '/admin/posts.php');
    return;
}
```

Here, all we've added is two new session variables and their respective data, once the user, having logged, has been allowed access to the admin panel. Our application uses both of these session variables to deduce if the current user is logged in during their use of the application's admin panel, and to work out how active they are while using it.

Those are the only things we'll be changing in the `login.php` script, so next, let's take a look at the `admin.php` file that's also in our `includes` folder. To begin with, we're going to add to the `Adminpanel`'s constructor, as well as adding some code at the start of our file:

```php
<?php
session_start();
require_once 'database.php';
class Adminpanel {
    public function __construct() {
        $inactive = 600;
        if (isset($_SESSION["kickstart_login"])) {
            $sessionTTL = time() - $_SESSION["timeout"];
            if ($sessionTTL > $inactive) {
                session_unset();
                session_destroy();
                header("Location: http://" . $_SERVER['SERVER_NAME']
 . "/login.php?status=inactive");
            }
        }
        $_SESSION["timeout"] = time();
        $login = $_SESSION['kickstart_login'];
        if (empty($login)) {
            session_unset();
            session_destroy();
            header('Location: http://'.$_SERVER['SERVER_NAME']
.'/login.php?status=loggedout');
        } else {
            $this->ksdb = new Database;
            $this->base - (object) '';
            $this->base->url = 'http://'.$_SERVER['SERVER_NAME'];
        }
    }
}
```

To begin with, we've added the session_start() function at the top of our file to begin the session each time a user's browser requests a page within the admin panel. Then, with the code we've added to the constructor, our Adminpanel class checks first to see how active our user's been throughout the admin panel, and if they've become idle, our application logs them out by killing their session and returning them to the login screen. If they're still active, the class will then check to see if the user has made a request to log out, or if they are trying to access the admin panel directly without logging in first. In either case, the user will be redirected back to the login screen to log in. Finally, if the user has already logged in and has an active session, the class will start to load up everything it needs to render the admin panel correctly.

Next, let's look at the `Posts` class, which extends the `Adminpanel` class:

```php
public function __construct() {
    parent::__construct();
    if (!empty($_GET['action'])) {
        switch ($_GET['action']) {
            case 'create':
                $this->addPost();
                break;
            default:
                $this->listPosts();
                break;
            case 'save':
                $this->savePost();
                break;
            case 'delete':
                $this->deletePost();
                break;
        }
    } else {
        $this->listPosts();
    }
}
```

Here, we've added a new case in the `switch` conditional. This checks whether the `action` URL variable contains the string `delete`. If so, our application then needs to load up a new method titled `deletePost()`. So let's go ahead and add that method into the bottom of the class now:

```php
public function deletePost() {
    if (!empty($_GET['id']) && is_numeric($_GET['id'])) {
        $query = "DELETE FROM `posts` WHERE id = ?"
        $stmt = $this>db->prepare($query);
        $stmt->execute(array($_GET['id']));
        $delete = $stmt->rowCount();
        $this->db = null;
        if (!empty($delete) && $delete > 0) {
            header("Location: " . $this->base->url .
➥"/posts.php?delete=success");
        } else {
            header("Location: " . $this->base->url .
➥"/posts.php?delete=error");
```

```
            }
        }
    }
```

Above, we've added the functionality required to allow us to delete posts with the **Delete** action button (which we see when the admin panel lists all of our posts). To do this, not only have we added the required functionality to the `deletePost()` method, but we've also added the code in the `Posts` constructor necessary to detect the `delete` method when it's requested in the URL. We've done this by adding a new `switch case` in the `Posts` constructor to identify from the URL variable which action we want to take with the post we've selected from the admin panel. We've also added functionality in both the constructor and `editPosts()` method to allow us to edit posts that have already been created.

Finally, we need to update the `savePost()` method:

```
public function savePost() {
    $array = $format = $return = array();
    if (!empty($_POST['post'])) {
        $post = $_POST['post'];
    }
    if (!empty($post['content'])) {
        $array['content'] = $post['content'];
        $format[] = ':content';
    }
    $cols = $values = '';
    $i=0;
    foreach ($array as $col => $data) {
        if ($i == 0) {
            $cols .= $col;
            $values .= $format[$i];
        } else {
            $cols .= ','.$col;
            $values .= ','.$format[$i];
        }
        $i++;
    }
    try {
        // This query has an SQL injection vulnerability
        $query = $this->ksdb->db->prepare("INSERT INTO posts
➥(".$cols.") VALUES (".$values.")");
        for ($c = 0; $c < $i; $c++) {
```

```
            $query->bindParam($format[$c], ${'var'.$c});
        }
        $z=0;
        foreach ($array as $col => $data) {
            ${'var' . $z} = $data;
            $z++;
        }
        $result = $query->execute();
        $add = $query->rowCount();
    } catch (PDOException $e) {
        echo $e->getMessage();
    }
    $query->closeCursor();
    $this->db = null;
    if (!empty($add)) {
        $status = array('success' => 'Your post has been saved
➥successfully.');
    } else {
        $status = array('error' => 'There has been an error saving
➥your post. Please try again later.');
    }
    header("Location: http://localhost/kickstart/admin/posts.php");
}
```

Our update to the savePost() method enables our application to handle an extra
field when we create or edit our posts. This new field allows us to enter a title for
our blog posts. Until now, our blog post titles have been nothing more than unique
id numbers. However, since we've now created a new field for our blog post, this
means we need to add a new column to our posts table inside our database, which
you'll need to do either through a MySQL query or by using the phpMyAdmin GUI
interface. It's recommended that you set this column to have the type of VARCHAR,
and a length of around 100. This should allow plenty of room to write any title they
wish. Once this is done, your posts table should look like Figure 5.1.

#	Name	Type	Collation	Attributes	Null	Default	Extra	Action
1	**id**	int(11)			No	None	AUTO_INCREMENT	Change ● Drop ▼ More
2	**content**	longtext	latin1_swedish_ci		No	None		Change ● Drop ▼ More
3	**title**	varchar(250)	latin1_swedish_ci		No	None		Change ● Drop ▼ More

Figure 5.1. Our posts table

The next step is for us to update the template **manageposts.php**:

```php
<?php require_once '_inc/header.php'; ?>
<a href="<?php echo $this->base->url . '/posts.php?action=create';
➥ ?>" class="btn btn-info">Create Post</a>
<a href="<?php echo $this->base->url . '/comments.php'; ?>" class=
➥"btn btn-info">Comments</a>
<table>
    <thead>
        <tr>
            <td>Post Title</td>
            <td>Post Content</td>
            <td>Actions</td>
        </tr>
    </thead>
    <tbody>
    <?php foreach($posts as $post): ?>
        <tr>
            <td><h3><?php echo (!empty($post['title']) ?
➥htmlspecialchar($post['title']) : 'Post #' . htmlspecialchar
➥($post['id'])); ?></h3></td>
            <td><p><?php echo implode(' ', array_slice(explode(' ',
➥ strip_tags($post['content'])), 0, 10)); ?> [...]</p></td>
            <td><a href="<?php echo $this->base->url . "/posts.php
➥?id=" . $post['id'] . "&action=edit"; ?>" class="btn btn-primary">
➥Edit Post</a><a href="<?php echo $this->base->url . "/posts.php?
➥id=" . $post['id'] . "&action=delete"; ?>" class="btn btn-primary
➥">Delete Post</a></td>
        </tr>
    <?php endforeach; ?>
    </tbody>
</table>
<?php require_once '_inc/footer.php'; ?>
```

Now our template file has an added field, in which we can add titles for our posts. It will connect with the code we've added in the savePost() method, so the data can be added to the database.

We also need to add this new title field to the **newpost.php** template, which we use to create our posts. The file should now look like this:

```php
<?php require_once '_inc/header.php'; ?>
<form action="<?php echo $this->base->url . '/posts.php?action=save'
➥; ?>" class="row" method="POST">
    <section class="span7">
        <h3>New Post</h3>
        <div class="control-group">
            <label class="control-label" for="content">Title</label>
            <div class="controls">
                <input type="text" name="post[title]" id="title"
➥placeholder="Your Post Title" />
            </div>
        </div>
        <div class="control-group">
            <label class="control-label" for="wmd-input">Content
➥</label>
            <div class="wmd-panel controls">
                <div id="wmd-button-bar"></div>
                <textarea class="wmd-input" name="post[content]"
➥   id="wmd-input">*Start Typing Here*</textarea>
            </div>
        </div>
        <div class="control-group">
            <div class="controls">
                <button type="submit" class="btn">Save Post</button>
            </div>
        </div>
    </section>
    <section class="span4" style="padding-left:20px; border-left:1px
➥ solid #eee;">
        <div id="wmd-preview" class="wmd-panel wmd-preview"></div>
    </section>
</form>
<?php require_once '_inc/footer.php'; ?>
```

In addition to adding an extra field for the user to insert a title to their posts, we've also changed the text area where they enter the content; we've changed it so that it has become a markdown-aware input field. For those unfamiliar with markdown[4], it's a simple plain text markup syntax designed to make it easy to add formatting to content. A markdown engine then converts the content to use valid HTML formatting.

---

[4] http://daringfireball.net/projects/markdown/

For our project, we're going to use an easy-to-implement JavaScript Markdown converter and editor called Pagedown[5]. To implement the library you need to load the three Pagedown libraries: `Markdown.Converter`, `Markdown.Sanitizer` and `Markdown.Editor`, in that order. Once you have these libraries loaded, you initialize the libraries by adding the following code to the `<head>` tag in your **header.php** template file:

```
<script>
    (function () {
        var converter = new Markdown.Converter();
        var editor = new Markdown.Editor(converter);
        editor.run();
    }());
</script>
```

You will also need to ensure you have the correct elements to load up the editor's format buttons, as well as giving your text area the correct class for the libraries to work out where to load the text format code. In addition, the libraries need to know where to display the preview of your post while you type in the content and the formatting.

We've already added both of these elements and their required classes to the template above. let;s take a look at the code we added. Here's the code for the formatting buttons and text entry :

```
<div class="wmd-panel controls">
    <div id="wmd-button-bar"></div>
        <textarea class="wmd-input" name="post[content]"
➥id="wmd-input">*Start Typing Here*</textarea>
</div>
```

And the code for the preview area:

---

[5] http://code.google.com/p/pagedown/

```
<section class="span4" style="padding-left:20px; border-left:1px
➥solid #eee;">
    <div id="wmd-preview" class="wmd-panel wmd-preview"></div>
</section>
```

You can identify which areas are required by the Pagedown libraries by looking for elements that have the prefix wmd before their ids and/or classes. Once these libraries are loaded, you should be able to start typing your post content, as well as some markdown formatting, into the editor area, as shown in Figure 5.2.

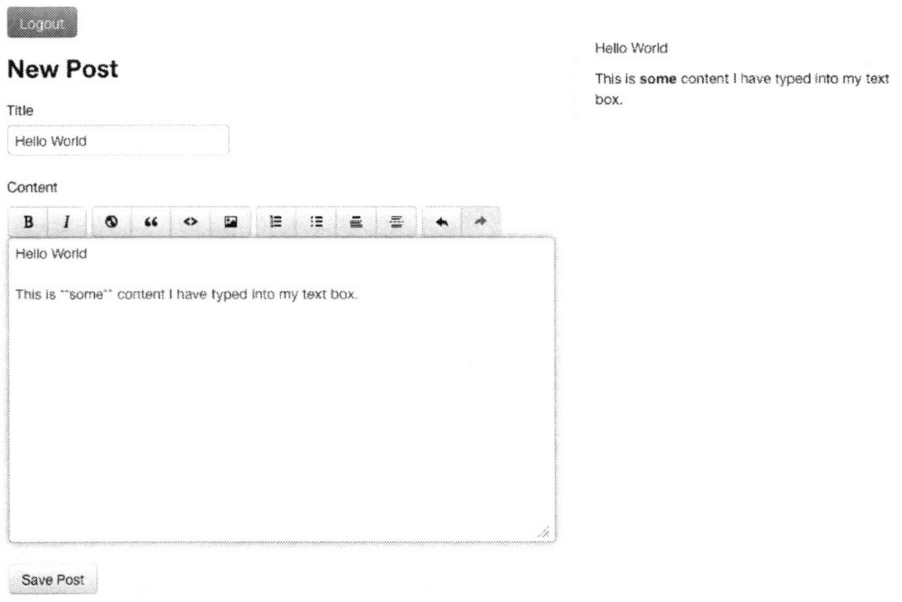

Logout

New Post

Title

Hello World

Content

| B | *I* | ⊘ | " | <> | 🖼 | ☰ | ☷ | ☰ | ☰ | ↰ | ↱ |

Hello World

This is **some** content I have typed into my text box.

Save Post

Hello World

This is **some** content I have typed into my text box.

Figure 5.2. Writing a post in the text editor

You should also notice that we have a new button added to the top of the template file called **Comments**. This new button, when clicked, will take the user to a comment management panel where they can view all the comments added to our posts, as well as delete comments they don't want on the blog. To get this running, what we need to do first is to create a new table in our database where users' comments will be stored. Set up a new table in your database as shown in Figure 5.3.

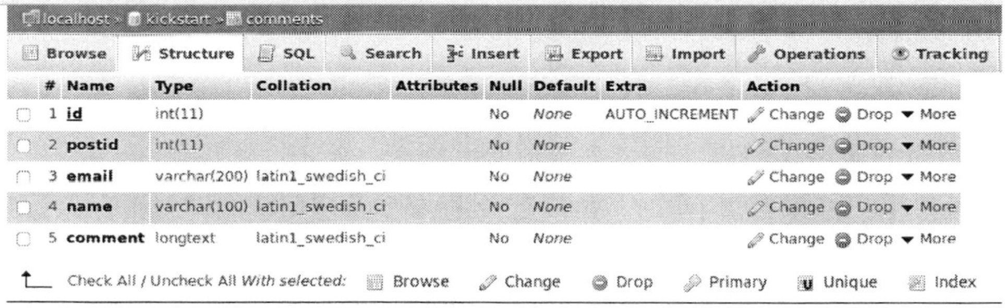

#	Name	Type	Collation	Attributes	Null	Default	Extra	Action
1	id	int(11)			No	None	AUTO_INCREMENT	Change Drop More
2	postid	int(11)			No	None		Change Drop More
3	email	varchar(200)	latin1_swedish_ci		No	None		Change Drop More
4	name	varchar(100)	latin1_swedish_ci		No	None		Change Drop More
5	comment	longtext	latin1_swedish_ci		No	None		Change Drop More

Figure 5.3. Our `comments` table

To get this section of the admin panel up and running, let's open up our **admin.php** file in the includes folder again and amend the code to the constructor to begin with:

```
public function __construct() {
    parent::__construct();
    if (!empty($_GET['action']) && $_GET['action'] == 'delete') {
        $this->deleteComment();
    } else {
        $this->listComments();
    }
}
```

As we can see, our constructor now checks for a URL variable title `action` and checks if the variable exists, and if it holds the string `delete`. If so, our application will load up the `deleteComment()` method, and if not, it'll load the `listComments()` method. So let's build these methods, starting with `listComments()`:

```
public function listComments() {
    $comments = $return = array();
    $query = $this->ksdb->db->prepare("SELECT * FROM comments");
    try {
        $query->execute();
        for ($i = 0; $row = $query->fetch(); $i++) {
            $return[$i] = array();
            foreach ($row as $key => $rowitem) {
                $return[$i][$key] = $rowitem;
            }
        }
    } catch (PDOException $e) {
        echo $e->getMessage();
```

```
    }
    $comments = $return;
    require_once 'templates/managecomments.php';
}
```

In this method, our application loads up all the comments from the comments table in our database using PDO. Once the comments are collected from the database, they're loaded into an array with a unique key for each comment. If there's a problem connecting to the database, or with our database PDO query, our application will fire back an error message. Finally, the method loads up the template file manage-comments.php. Now we just need to create the deleteComment() method:

```
public function deleteComment() {
    if (!empty($_GET['id']) && is_numeric($_GET['id'])) {
        $query = "DELETE FROM `comments` WHERE id = ?";
        $stmt = $this->db->prepare($query);
        $stmt->execute(array($_GET['id']));
        $delete = $result->rowCount();
        $this->db = null;
        if(!empty($delete) && $delete > 0){
            header("Location: ".$this->base->url."/
➥comments.php?delete=success");
        }else{
            header("Location: ".$this->base->url."/
➥comments.php?delete=error");
        }
    }
}
```

Our deleteComment() method is very similar to our deletePost() method from the Posts class except, this time, our application is looking for the URL variable id to contain the id of the comment in relation to its row in our database. We also have a if conditional statement to redirect back to the admin's comments panel with the correct status message—success or error—to let the user know if the attempt to delete a comment has worked or not.

Our next step is to create our template to list the comments in our admin panel, which we will title managecomments.php. Once we've created this file, we need to add the following code to our template:

```php
<?php require_once '_inc/header.php'; ?>
<a href="<?php echo $this->base->url . '/posts.php?action=create';
➥?>" class="btn btn-info">Create Post</a>
<a href="<?php echo $this->base->url . '/comments.php'; ?>"
➥class="btn btn-info">Comments</a>
<table cellpadding="10">
    <thead>
        <tr>
            <td>Commenter</td>
            <td>Post ID</td>
            <td>Comment</td>
            <td>Actions</td>
        </tr>
    </thead>
    <tbody>
    <?php foreach($comments as $comment): ?>
        <tr>
            <td><h4><?php echo htmlspecialchar($comment['name']);
➥ ?></h4></td>
            <td><p><?php echo htmlspecialchar($comment['email']);
➥ ?></p></td>
            <td><p><?php echo htmlspecialchar($comment['comment']);
➥ ?></p></td>
            <td><a href="<?php echo $this->base->url . "/comments.
➥php?id=" . htmlspecialchar($comment['id']) . "&action=delete";
➥?>" class="btn btn-primary">Delete Comment</a></td>
        </tr>
    <?php endforeach; ?>
    </tbody>
</table>
<?php require_once '_inc/footer.php'; ?>
```

With that code added, you should now have a working admin panel, as shown in Figure 5.4. Feel free to use the admin panel to create some posts.

Figure 5.4. Our admin panel in action

Once you've finished testing your admin panel, it's time to add the finishing touches to our blog platform, and start creating the final functionality for the front-end section of our project.

First, we need to add a new library to our front end so that the public side of our blog converts the markdown formatting into valid HTML. To do this, we add Michel Fortin's PHP markdown library[6]. This is very easy to install and will render our markdown perfectly, plus it's written in pure PHP, so we don't need to worry about installing additional software on our server. We just need to call the library when we want to convert markdown formatting to HTML.

Download the library and move the **markdown.php** file to the `includes` directory within your project's main directory. Next, open up the main **posts.php** file from your project's `includes` directory and insert the following code:

```php
public function viewpost($postid) {
    $id = $postid;
    $posts = $this->ksdb->dbselect('posts', array('*'), array('id'
=> $id));
    $markdown = new Michelf\Markdown();
    $posts[0]['content'] = $markdown->defaultTransform($posts[0][
'content']);
    $postcomments = $this->comments->getcomments($posts[0]['id']);
```

---

[6] http://michelf.ca/projects/php-markdown/

```
    $template = 'view-post.php';
    include_once 'frontend/templates/'.$template;
}
```

We've included the new markdown library at the start of our script, ready for us to use when the application needs to render data in the markdown format. We've also changed the functionality in our `getposts()` method, as well as our `viewpost()` method, and we are now loading our `Comments` class in our constructor.

Let's start by looking a little closer at the code we've added to the two methods. In `getposts()` we've added a new `foreach` loop, which will call the `commentnumber()` method in our `Comments` class. We still need to add this method into the class, so let's keep that in mind and take a quick look at the `viewpost()` method. Here, we're loading the `markdown` class from the markdown library, and attributing this class to the variable `$markdown`, turning it into an object.

You'll notice the call to the markdown library is quite different from how we have called classes before; that is because Michel has used a **namespace** in his library. A namespace helps to establish a unique identifier for a class. This avoids potential clashing when two classes are loaded with the same name. Namespacing was introduced in PHP 5.3. It's a feature that is starting to gain popularity, as it helps to solve naming complications when creating libraries for public use. Namespaces can be applied to classes like so:

```php
<?php
namespace Project;
class myProject {
    function index() {
        echo 'Loading a method from a class with a namespace!';
    }
}
```

They're very simple to implement, but can make a huge improvement to code interoperability. For example, the markdown PHP library is using the namespace `Michelf`, so to load the library's class and its methods into our scripts, we just need to have the namespace appear in our script before we call the class. In this case, instead of writing:

```
$markdown = new Markdown();
```

we have to write:

```php
$markdown = new Michelf\Markdown();
```

 More on Namespaces

For more information on namespaces, please see the PHP manual[7] and this article on SitePoint[8].

Now that we have our markdown PHP library implemented, we can use it to transform posts that are written in markdown syntax into fully rendered HTML.

The last new piece of code we've added is a call to another method in our Comments class, which we've yet to code. This method is getcomments(), which will get our application to load up all the comments for a specific post.

Let's start by opening up the **comments.php** file from within the "frontend" directory. Amend the code as follows:

```php
<?php
require_once 'frontend/posts.php';
class Comments extends Blog {
    public function __construct() {
        parent::__construct();
        if ($_SERVER['REQUEST_METHOD'] === 'POST' && !empty($_POST[
➥'comment'])) {
            $this->addcomment();
        }
    }
}
```

Our constructor for this class loads everything we need from the parent class's constructor (which is the constructor from the Blog class) then checks to see if there's a post request to submit a new comment. If there is, the application will then fire the addcomment() method. This method is where we take all the data posted from the comments form and prepare it for entry into our comments database using the dbadd() method from the PDO database library.

---

[7] http://php.net/manual/en/language.namespaces.php
[8] http://www.sitepoint.com/php-namespaces/

```
public function commentnumber($postid) {
        $query = $this->ksdb->dbselect('comments', array('*'),
➥ array('postid' => $postid));
        $commentnum = count($query);
        if ($commentnum <= 0) {
            $commentnum = 0;
        }
        return $commentnum;
    }
    public function getcomments($postid) {
        return $this->ksdb->dbselect('comments', array('*'), array
➥('postid' => $postid));
    }
```

You can also see we have our method `getcomments()`, which requires that a variable
containing a post id is passed to the method. Any data that needs to be passed to a
method before it can be processed correctly, can be placed in parentheses after the
method name. The method collects all the comments attributed to a post based on
the id passed to the method, and returns them to the variable attributed when this
method was called. This means that if data is passed to the method, PHP will throw
an error:

```
public function addcomment() {
        $status= '';
        $array = $format = array();
        if (!empty($_POST['comment'])) {
            $comment = $_POST['comment'];
        }
        if (!empty($comment['fullname'])) {
            $array['name'] = $comment['fullname'];
            $format[] = ':fullname';
        }
        if (!empty($comment['email'])) {
            $array['email'] = $comment['email'];
            $format[] = ':email';
        }
        if (!empty($comment['context'])) {
            $array['comment'] = $comment['context'];
            $format[] = ':context';
        }
        if (!empty($comment['postid'])) {
            $array['postid'] = $comment['postid'];
            $format[] = ':postid';
```

```
        }
        $add = $this->ksdb->dbadd('comments', $array, $format);
        if (!empty($add) && $add > 0) {
            $status = array('success' => 'Your comment has been
➥submitted');
            $key = 'success';
        } else {
            $status = array('error' => 'There has been an error
➥submitting your comment. Please try again later.');
            $key = 'error';
        }
        header('http://localhost/kickstart/?id=' . $comment['postid']);
    }
}
```

We also have the `commentnumber()` method, which requires a post id to be passed to it before it can be executed. This counts all the comments that are attached to the post id passed to the method, and returns this number.

We now have the `Comments` class up and running. All we need to do is tweak our **list-posts.php** template to show how many comments our posts have—as well as the post's new titles—and add a section in our **view-post.php** template to allow visitors to submit comments (and again, show the new post title).

Let's start with the **list-posts.php** file. Open it and add the following code:

```
<?php require_once 'includes/temps/header.php'; ?>
<?php foreach ($posts as $post): ?>
    <h3><?php echo (!empty($post['title']) ? htmlspecialchar($post
➥['title']) : 'Post #' . htmlspecialchar($post['id'])); ?></h3>
        <p><?php echo implode(' ', array_slice(explode(' ',
➥strip_tags($post['content'])), 0, 10)); ?> [...]</p>
        <a href="<?php echo $this->base->url . "/?id=" . $post['id']
➥; ?>" class="btn btn-primary">Read More</a><p>comments: <?php echo
➥ $post['comments']; ?></p>
    <hr/>
```

```
<?php endforeach; ?>

<?php require_once 'includes/temps/footer.php'; ?>
```

Now we have a small section, which shows the number of comments each post has, as well as the post's title and a short excerpt of each post's content each time it's listed.

Finally, let's add to our **view-post.php** template:

```
<?php require_once 'includes/temps/header.php'; ?>
<br/>
<a href="<?php echo $this->base->url; ?>" class="btn btn-primary">
➥Return to Post List</a>
<article>
<?php foreach($posts as $post): ?>
    <h3><?php echo (!empty($post['title']) ? htmlspecialchar($post
➥['title']) : 'Post #' . htmlspecialchar($post['id'])); ?></h3>
        <?php echo $post['content']; ?>
    <hr/>
<?php endforeach; ?>
<h3>Comments</h3>
<?php foreach ($postcomments as $comment): ?>
    <section class="span3">
        <figure>
            <img src="http://www.gravatar.com/avatar/<?php echo md5
➥($comment['email']); ?>" alt="">
        </figure>
        <h4><?php echo htmlspecialchar($comment['name']); ?></h4>
        <p><small><?php echo htmlspecialchar($comment['email']); ?>
➥</small></p>
    </section>
    <section class="span8">
        <p><?php echo htmlspecialchar($comment['comment']); ?></p>
    </section>
    <hr style="clear:both;"/>
<?php endforeach; ?>
<br/>
```

In this code, we've added a section that now displays the post title at the top of each post, as well as an area that shows each submitted comment. I should note that, when adding the section to show the blog post title, there's a conditional to check if the blog post has a title. If not, our script will display the blog post number, as well as the string "`Post #`", to give each post a fallback title in case it hasn't been given one. It's important to make sure that, when you're calling data in your scripts that may not always be there, you have a fallback so PHP doesn't display errors on your live site or application.

```
<h3>Leave Comment</h3>
<form action="<?php echo htmlspecialchars($_SERVER['PHP_SELF']); ?>"
➥method="post" class="form-horizontal">
    <input type="hidden" value="<?php echo $_GET['id']; ?>" name=
➥"comment[postid]" />
    <div class="control-group <?php echo (!empty($error)? 'error':
➥ ''); ?>">
        <label class="control-label" for="email">Email</label>
        <div class="controls">
            <input type="email" name="comment[email]" id="email"
➥placeholder="Your Email Address"/>
        </div>
    </div>
    <div class="control-group <?php echo (!empty($error) ? 'error' :
➥ ''); ?>">
        <label class="control-label" for="name">Full Name</label>
        <div class="controls">
            <input type="text" name="comment[fullname]" id="name"
➥placeholder="Your Full Name"/>
        </div>
    </div>
    <div class="control-group <?php echo (!empty($error) ? 'error' :
➥ ''); ?>">
        <label class="control-label" for="comment">Comment</label>
        <div class="controls">
            <textarea id="comment" name="comment[context]">
➥</textarea>
        </div>
    </div>
    <div class="control-group">
        <div class="controls">
            <button type="submit" class="btn">Submit Comment
➥</button>
        </div>
    </div>
```

```
</form>
</article>
<?php require_once('includes/temps/footer.php'); ?>
```

In our code above, we've added a brand new form for visitors to the blog to leave a comment on a blog post. The form will submit the data—using the post method—to itself where our application will then be able to process the data, and save it to the database using the addComment() method. We've also added if statements for each of the input fields in the form in case the user has forgotten to fill in a field when they tried to submit their comment. We also have a hidden field, which holds the id of the post—something we need in order to save the comment to the database correctly.

 Using Gravatar for User Avatars

One thing to note is that we have added a link to Gravatar[9] to place the user's avatar next to the comment. Gravatar is a free service, which allows users to upload an avatar image to an online server and attribute their personal email address to it. This enables developers to code into their applications a call to the Gravatar server to collect an avatar that may be connected to a user's email address they've been supplied with.

The call to the Gravatar server is free, and means you don't have to store avatar images yourself. Gravatar's goal is to provide a quick and easy solution to keep everyone's avatars up to date and consistent. If a user doesn't have an avatar set on Gravatar, it will return a default blank avatar instead. Each email address is encoded using a basic method, so we're required to encode the user's email address using md5 encryption; we've done this in our code in order to retrieve the avatar from Gravatar's servers.

---

[9] http://en.gravatar.com/

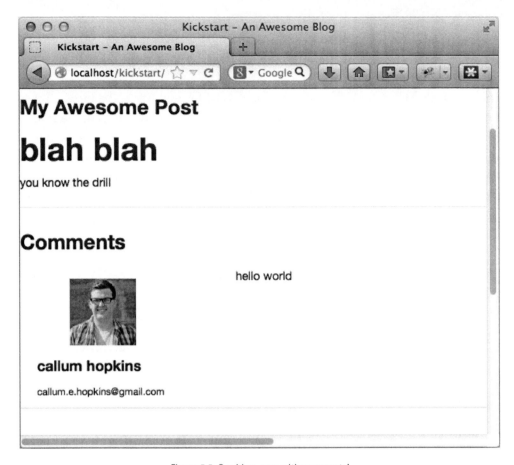

Figure 5.5. Our blog, now with comments!

Returning to our code, at the bottom of our template, we have a new form area where users can enter data about themselves, as well as submitting a comment to be attached and displayed on the blog post.

Now all we need to do is save this template and we should have a fully working blog platform complete with comments, as shown in Figure 5.5. Congratulations!

Summary

Sessions and cookies are vital when you want to add user accounts into a PHP application. They are powerful developer tools for personalizing data displayed in the browser, as they can quickly and effectively identity users through data stored on the user's computer. For user accounts in applications, cookies and sessions are vital to create logged in statuses, which we have implemented for our admin panel in our application. However, it's important to remember the potential security risks that come with using cookies and sessions, and it's also important to implement code that will reduce the security risk.

For more information on using sessions and cookies, please see the following articles:

- http://www.sitepoint.com/php-sessions/

- http://www.sitepoint.com/baking-cookies-in-php/

- http://www.php.net/manual/en/book.session.php

- http://php.net/manual/en/features.cookies.php

Now that we have a working blog platform, we're about to enter the final chapter. There, we'll look at different areas in PHP where we can improve security, and where we could potentially add parts to our blog platform were we to extend the application's functionality and processing.

Chapter 6

PHP and Security

Testing and security are two of the most important elements of application development. You may be able to create the most impressive application ever seen, but if you don't ensure that it's bug free and secure from attackers, you're not finishing the job.

In this chapter we'll be covering some basic methods to improve the security of your PHP applications. It'd be impossible to cover every single possible implementation in this short book, so it's also a good idea to check out the extra reading resources provided, to build upon the techniques covered in this chapter.

php.ini and Security

We can start planting the seeds of sound security before we even start to build anything in PHP. At the beginning of the book, we briefly touched on the PHP configuration file **php.ini**. It enables us to configure a lot of PHP's behaviors, such as how it handles file uploads, performs script caching, and, of particular interest to us now, handling PHP's security.

Meddle at Your Own Risk!

Do not edit any settings if you are not 100% confident about how the changes will impact your PHP installation. Diving in head first and editing settings without knowing what you're doing could result in unexpected functioning.

Uneditable php.ini

Certain hosting providers may not let you access or edit the **php.ini** file. If you can't access the directory in which the file is located, you should contact your host and ask about making changes.

To locate your **php.ini** file, use the `phpinfo()` function to discover its location. Need a quick refresher? We did this before in Chapter 1.

Once you've found the correct file, open it up in your text editor and you'll see a huge amount of configuration options available. A handful of these, discussed below, will help improve the security of your application.

allow_url_include

```
allow_url_include=Off
```

By default, the standard PHP installation has `allow_url_include` turned off, but some hosting providers may have it turned on so it's important to check your **php.ini** file.

With `allow_url_include` turned off, PHP can only load and execute other files that reside on the web server's file system. However, if you activate `allow_url_include`, you can include additional files via URL. This may seem like an interesting and possibly useful feature to have turned on, but doing opens up your application to the possibility of malicious code injection attacks. For this reason it's highly recommended that this option remains turned off.

Code Injection

Code injection is the term used to describe when unwanted code from an external source is placed into a PHP script without consent. For more information on code injection, please see these external sources:

- http://www.theserverpages.com/articles/webmasters/php/security/Code_Injection_Vulnerabilities_Explained.html

- https://www.owasp.org/index.php/Code_Injection

A related setting is `allow_url_fopen` which should also be switched off.

open_basedir

```
open_basedir=/path/to/web/directory
```

Like `allow_url_include`, `open_basedir` can also help restrict files that scripts are allowed to load on the server. With `open_basedir`, you can set which directory files can be loaded from, and ensure that no file from outside that directory can be loaded in any scripts.

One method would-be attackers attempt is to access the **/etc/password** file on a Linux-based web server, which lists the registered user accounts on the server. If your PHP application is run from **/var/www**, you can set `open_basedir` to "/var/www/". Once set, files outside of the **www** directory cannot be included in your scripts, stopping attackers in their tracks. Enable this option when your application goes live to add an extra level of security to your server.

Error Management

During the development phase of a project it's useful to have PHP give you feedback when it encounters any errors or problems in your code. However, once your application is deployed, you really want these errors to be few and far between. Developers will want to hide PHP error messages from the users because, if these errors are seen they can give a sense of unreliability that impacts customer confidence.

Importantly, error messages can also give away vital information about your system's configuration, which hackers can use to their advantage. PHP's default error messages can contain information such as the application's installation path, database connection details, database column names, and other script details such as class names, object IDs, and variable names.

To ensure this information is hidden from users, set the `display_errors` option in **php.ini** to off. This tells PHP not to show errors during runtime when one occurs. It doesn't mean that PHP will ignore the error—rather that it won't display it in the browser.

You can still tell PHP to save any errors to a special log file, which you, the application developer, can refer to in privacy. To do this, set the `error_log` option to a path that's the location of the desired error log file.

It's also a good idea to turn the `log_errors` option on. This ensures that PHP will log errors, save the error data, and avoid all possibilities of rendering the error messages on the screen.

With these options set, PHP will privately create error logs for you to refer to when needed.

Improving Session Security

Sessions, as discussed in the previous chapter, are a means of temporarily storing data, such as whether a user is logged in or not. We're using sessions in our blog application and, as you have probably noted already, they provide useful functionality. Sessions may often only hold a small amount of data, but any piece of data related to gaining access to an application could potentially be gold dust to any attacker or hacker. By default, sessions store information about your application's users, and use cookies to help programming languages such as PHP match each users with the correct session information. Unfortunately, sessions maintain the login state that the attacker wants to achieve, which makes sessions one of the most attractive targets for hackers.

One way that hackers can try to hijack a session is to access the session data itself. Fortunately, **php.ini** comes to the rescue again and offers us the ability to change the location in which the sessions data is kept through the option `session.save_path`:

```
session.save_path = /var/lib/php
```

The example written above is the default. If you change the location, it will throw hackers off the scent as they'll need to figure out where you've relocated the session data to.

It's important to remember that, when you change this path, you ensure your web server can read and write to the new location. Fail to do this and your PHP won't be able to use sessions correctly, and will throw up errors!

Hackers will also often try to exploit your application and server through a technique known as Cross Site Scripting[1] (**XSS** for short), which allows them to inject malicious JavaScript code into your application. Sessions are often the target in XSS attacks and, if successful, they can do a variety of damage, from keyboard watching (where a script notes down all the keys pressed, including those pressed for passwords and login details) to forcing unauthorized advertisements ion your users for an attacker's financial gain. To help prevent XSS attacks, you can use the following option:

```
session.cookie_httponly = 1
```

This option, when set to 1—as is the default in most **php.ini** files—will restrict JavaScript from accessing cookies that have been created by PHP or for use with sessions. It's highly advised that you turn this option on if you don't intend JavaScript to use any data from cookies created in PHP, as it really does help to control the flow of data from the client's computer to your application and the server upon which it's hosted.

For more information on options within php.ini and how to make your PHP more secure, please see the following sources:

- http://www.sitepoint.com/a-tour-of-php-ini/

- http://php.net/manual/en/ini.php

- http://www.madirish.net/?article=229

---

[1] https://en.wikipedia.org/wiki/Cross-site_scripting

Validating Submitted Data

One of the biggest threats to PHP applications is not the lack of protection from attackers, but rather the threat of bad data submitted by users. Whether a user submits incorrect data on purpose or by accident is often difficult to work out, but incorrectly formatted data can harm your application.

It's important to ensure your users know what type of data they're supposed to submit. Use the correct input elements for the type of data you're prompting for, and make sure the labels clearly indicate what is expected.

Also, it's best practice to assume that, even if they have interacted with specifically restrictive input fields in your HTML form, users may still submit data that's formatted incorrectly. When the data is sent to your PHP script to be processed, it's important to implement some type of validating script.

There are several PHP functions we can use for validation. The following code example has been designed to check data that has been submitted by the user to see if the correct data has been provided, helping to ensure that it's in a format that can be used readily by the application:

```php
<?php
$input = array();
// this is where all of the filtered data will be stored

// an input field with the name 'number'
 that accepts only numeric input
if (isset($_POST['number']) && is_numeric($_POST['input'])) {
    $input['number'] = $_POST['number'];
}
// an input field with the name 'date' that accepts
 a dd/mm/yyyy date
if (isset($_POST['date'])) {
    list ($dd, $mm, $yyyy) = explode('/', $input);
    if (checkdate ($mm,$dd,$yyyy)) {
        $input['date'] = $_POST['date'];
    }
}
// an input field with the name 'content' that accepts
arbitrary text
if (isset($_POST['content'])) {
```

```
    // filter out any harmful HTML that may be in the string
    $input['content'] = strip_tags($_POST['content']);
}

// values in $input are safe to use in the application
```

In the example above, we inspect each of the incoming form values and place them into a new array if they pass some basic validation checks. Those that fail are not added to the $input array.

The is_numeric() function checks the contents of a string and will return true only if it contains characters that make up a number. Numeric strings consist of an optional leading sign (+ or -), any number of digits, and optionally a decimal part or exponential part.

The checkdate() function checks the validity of the a given date and will return true only if the arguments make up a valid date.

Finally, strip_tags() returns a string with HTML and PHP tags removed, leaving only basic formatting HTML tags (such as line break <br> tags) and plain text.

At the end of our validation checks, the values in $input can be used safely throughout the rest of our application knowing that they're in the correct format.

However, forms are not the only type of data for which we need to consider implementing validation. In the blog application we've built in this book, we've used URL variables to load new sections of the application and execute specific scripts. URL variables are often targeted by attackers because they're easy to manipulate and can cause some very serious damage to apps that haven't implemented appropriate security measures.

We've already implemented a few security validation techniques in our application, especially where we used URL variables to dictate which method or functionality should be executed:

```
...
if (!empty($_GET['id']) && is_numeric($_GET['id'])) {

...
```

This example, taken from **admin/posts.php**, shows that we have the `is_numeric()` function in place to ensure that the application continues to process the method inside the `if` statement only if the required data from the URL is a number. It will ignore any other values someone may try to pass through the URL.

Summary

In this chapter we've seen a brief overview of PHP security and looked at some basic ways to avoid some of the most common vulnerabilities.

PHP security is a huge topic and we've only really scratched the surface here. It's recommended that, every time you write a new function, imagine how someone would be able to:

■ gain illicit access to any protected areas

■ disrupt, distort, or change data that the application is processing

■ break, alter, or effect in any negative way the process and/or functionality of the application

It's also always worth thinking, during development, that a user may submit incorrect or incorrectly-formatted data whenever user input is required. If you keep these things in mind when you develop, you'll be able protect yourself from many of the initial security problems your application may encounter.

For more information on implementing security methods, functionality, and scripts into your PHP applications, please see:

■ http://www.sitepoint.com/top-10-php-security-vulnerabilities/

■ http://www.sitepoint.com/php-security-blunders/

■ http://www.php-security.net/

Conclusion

In this short book we've had a brief taste of PHP development and created a simple blogging platform. Everything we've discussed has been carefully chosen to help inspire you to hone your PHP development skills.

This book should only be considered to be a starting point on your journey as a PHP developer. A great resource for furthering your PHP skills is SitePoint's PHP channel, http://www.sitepoint.com/php/, which offers a wide range of articles for the PHP developer.

> The function of good software is to make the complex appear to be simple. — Grady Booch

CPSIA information can be obtained at www.ICGtesting.com
Printed in the USA
BVOW01s0922021013

332715BV00004B/8/P

9 780987 467409